Practice What You Preached

by

Ron DeBock, Ph.D.

PRACTICE WHAT YOU PREACHED

Grateful acknowledgment is made to the following for permission to include material in this book:

Dr. Ward M. Tanneberg, author of "Let Light Shine Out," Copyright © 1977.

Kent Hamilton, Councilman, City of Milton, Washington.

President Don Johnson and Past President Dr. Arthur C. Jerstad, Rotary Club of Puyallup.

Library of Congress Catalog Card Number: 93-90373

ISBN 0-9636750-0-1 — ISBN 0-9636750-1-X (lim. ed.)

Second Edition

To order copies, see page 223.

Jacket design by Tim Hodgson

This book is dedicated

To Billy Graham

and

To Paul and Jan Crouch

and

To Oral Roberts

and others who were not afraid

to attempt something big for God.

Contents

PART II - PRACTICING

iii

Acknowledgments

John Dotson with Ron

If the late John Dotson had not thrown his arms around a teenager on the sidewalk in front of the Foursquare Gospel Church in Olympia, it is doubtful that any book of my life would be worth writing. May I say it directly to him, "Thanks to you, Brother Dotson, I found the full and joyous life you promised. Thanks for your Christ-like love which won that boy to the Lord!"

Others in their own way have inspired me to write this book, and I am thankful for them. For Donna, a caring, faithful and supportive wife who never stopped believing in me, though she did have doubts. For Gary, whose practical help with punctuation, spelling and grammar was a real blessing. He deserves a Ph.D. degree for "Putting his Dad" through! More important, it is great to have an only son with Gary's intellect doing business in the same offices with me.

For the late R. J. Carlson, long-time Superintendent of the Northwest District Council of the Assemblies of God, for being there to care, to understand and to help me at the crossroads. For the late Wesley Morton, former pastor of Puyallup First Assembly, a missionary, and a loving shepherd of his flock. For my current pastor, Sam Benson, who came to Puyallup with a vision for a strong assembly of believers, who put together the kind of pastoral staff that can make it happen. His messages inspire us all to let God do a work in our lives and to catch a vision for what we need to accomplish for the kingdom of God.

For Dr. Bob Moorehead, pastor of Overlake Christian Church in Kirkland, who inspired his congregation in twin collections on a single Sunday to give $1,596,309. I was curiously drawn to both services on that historic day, June 25, 1978. Seed-faith gifts from my heart (I was eager to be part of the festival of giving) led to a golden harvest in my life for months afterward. I'll never forget it! Pastor Moorehead personally led the way. Reflecting on the special day, he summed it up nicely during the evening worship, "We went broke for God!"

For Bart Clarke, Dick Crowe, Lory Kalles, Hermon Ray, Pat Robertson and Charles Stanley.

For Peter Toxby, a business associate who became a good friend on our 1985 holy land tour, for his helpful counsel and for his generous support of my *alma mater*, Northwest College in Kirkland, Washington. For Tom Slate, retired Methodist minister, whose proofreading and comments on the manuscript were invaluable. For Julie Christensen at Valley Press, for her technical skills on the Macintosh computer and for her tact in pointing out the errors in my copy.

Finally, my highest praise goes to the One who ordered my steps into abundance, adventure and joy, the Lord Jesus Christ.

Foreword

Randall K. Barton

Have you ever wondered at the way certain people look for the best in others and their circumstances? Dr. Ron DeBock possesses that special knack for God-inspired optimism! In his autobiography, the reader will find many key principles that can be mastered by anyone with the desire to positively influence others ... and in so doing experience the joys of life God has prepared for each of us.

"Practice What You Preached" teaches us as Christians to expect the best in life and to truly put into practice the Scripture that challenges us, "In everything give thanks: for this is the will of God in Christ Jesus concerning you" (II Thess. 5:18).

As a friend and colleague, I have found the author deeply committed to his family, church, work, community, alma mater and most importantly, his God. What more could someone say regarding the character of a Christian?

No matter what your current circumstances in life, the

adventure of living awaits your admission. This autobiography accounts one man's journey and perspective on that adventure. As you read about this journey, I believe that you will agree with me that Dr. Ron DeBock truly has put into practice in everyday living the truth that he preached.

Randall K. Barton, President
Assemblies of God Foundation

Introduction

Here's a question for you? Can you look back and see a special year in your life which stands out as being pivotal, or like a crossroads? Now if you are in your youth as you read this, it's probably too early for you to make such a discovery. On the other hand, if you're "over the hill" as I am, the search might prove to be interesting.

For me, the year was 1971!

Timing is a bigger factor in our lives than we like to think. It's a good idea to look back and reflect upon the past. Just so long as we are not guilty of living there constantly, of course.

In February of 1971, I was undergoing tests for my hearing at the Philadelphia Naval Hospital. A routine physical taken in January at the U. S. Naval Training Center at Great Lakes, Illinois, got me there. What began as routine tests became over two months' hospitalization, complete with all the tests, evaluations and in-patient care which navy hospitals are noted for.

The only certainty I enjoyed was that God was leading. The medics left the big decision up to me. To stay in or get out of the U. S. Navy.

I think there is something about me that you should know before we go any further. It is the significance I have learned to give to little indicators. These include the unusual, sometimes bordering on the miraculous, experiences which come my way.

You will meet a few of these encounters in this book. I call them "indicators" because in some way they indicate that God is leading. If that sounds mystical or corny, I can only remind you that it took a whole lifetime for me to recognize indicators for what they are. Here are two examples:

Ken Fukuda was a member of a Bible class I was teaching

at Puyallup First Assembly. A Japanese nisei born in Long Beach, California, Ken was a studious history buff. He bought all three of the suggested textbooks for the class. It was refreshing to have such a serious student!

At the close of one of those Sunday morning class sessions, Ken said that he would like to get together with me and discuss a matter of interest. He didn't mention the subject and I didn't ask. I agreed it would be fine to look at the matter together at some convenient time.

Weeks went by, even a few months. One day Ken and I met while at a local bakery. I had finished a bowl of soup. Ken got a soup "to go" as he was in a hurry to return to a remodelling job. We left together.

"By the way, Ken, what was it you wanted to talk about? It's about time we got together, don't you think?" I said.

"The thing I am curious about is the big difference in the ages of the men of the Old Testament before the flood and after the flood," Ken said, as he put his soup on a protruding cement ledge.

We stood there discussing the matter for several minutes. All of the while, Ken's soup was getting cold. But, I could see he was vastly more interested in our topic of conversation than in his lunch.

As we left the spot in front of the bakery, we agreed that it would be rare indeed for anyone to live to the ripe old age of Moses' 120 years.

"You may make it. You're younger than I am," Ken quipped.

"I'm not so sure. What year were you born?" I asked.

"1928. How about you?"

"1928! What month?" I asked.

We narrowed it down to the fact that Ken and I were born on 12 September 1928. Now, there's an indicator!

Less than a week later, I arose very early to prepare invitations to my fortieth anniversary as an ordained minister of the Assemblies of God. My thoughts during the day turned to gratitude to the Lord for the strength He gave me to complete this book. God had enabled me to carry on the day-today management duties and still find time to write. When evening came, I sat in my living room chair.

Trinity Broadcasting Network was playing on Channel 29. Donna and I have been avid fans and supporters of TBN for many years!

While watching that particular night, Tuesday, October 20, 1992, Jan Crouch asked viewers to write a letter to encourage her husband, Paul Crouch, to write the story of the ministry of Trinity Broadcasting Network. Jan said TBN's twentieth anniversary will be celebrated May 28, 1993. I happily sat down and got off a letter of encouragement to Paul Crouch!

Where's the indicator? Just this. In prayer before writing the letter to the founder of this great world-wide television ministry, I was faced with the fact that my own ministry pales into dwarf proportions by comparison. While my ministry may be twice as long as that of TBN, their amazing contacts with millions...well, you get the idea. No comparison!

Nevertheless, Donna and I can be partners in their ministry. We have the privilege of being a small part of a big ministry in these last days for persuading men.[1]

My decision to accept a medical discharge from the Navy would be the biggest vocational decision I would ever make. I should make it clear that my biggest personal decisions were to accept Christ and to accept the call to the ministry. But there is a vast difference between the choice of a free youth and the life-wrenching choice of a mature man to change his career.

Separation from the Navy in 1971 looked sadly like a separation from the ministry, my heavenly calling. But time revealed a new merger between the heavenly call and earthly service.

The year 1971 was, indeed, the crossroads. Roughly half of my life's work (ministry) took place **before** that time, and half of it **after** then. Obviously, such a neat division would not be known until I looked back on it twenty-one years later. I suppose one might argue that this book presents a case to show that the big decision was the right one. My own feeling at the time was that I was making the right decision. Looking back now on both of the 21-year segments of my life, let me tell you the story!

Essentially, the first half of my life was devoted to PREACHING. For reasons only further reading can explain, the second half seemed to fit quite properly into the classification of PRACTICING. Now you know where this book gets it's name. Almost.

"You have a severe hearing loss," the medical officer told me. "You can make your own decision about continuance on active duty."

Make that decision myself? I must have heard the doctor wrong! Funny, here I had been taking those audio tests for weeks. And for weeks I had been thinking how easy it will be to perceive the will of God in the matter of remaining in the navy chaplaincy or getting out. Continued active duty or medical discharge? Surely all of this was squarely in the hands of the navy medics. Isn't God good to make it so easy for me, I thought.

I looked at the doctor closely and asked him to please repeat what he had just said. He didn't seem to mind repeating it. (After all, why was I in the hospital in the first place?)

"The decision is yours," he reiterated. "Your hearing loss is not serious enough to disqualify you for continued active naval service. But, if you want a medical discharge, it will be granted. It's up to you."

The medical officer wore a gold leaf on his collar which identified him as a lieutenant commander in the medical corps. But his insignia might just as well have been a couple of stars in this case, I thought. (He was not only speaking for the Navy, he was speaking for God!). He told me I need not rush the important decision. Two weeks would be just fine.

Others were waiting for my decision, too. The Chief of Navy Chaplains for one. And in Springfield, Missouri, my church's Commission on Chaplains waited to hear what the Navy would do with me. Donna and our three children were waiting, too. Ah, the virtue of patience! Where does it come from? From tribulation, remember?[2]

I looked back on thirteen years of active duty, eleven as a Navy Chaplain and two years' enlisted service. The enlisted service might be facetiously described as a special assignment as Commander of an LSD (large steel desk) moored in the nation's capital, Washington, D. C. There's nothing like starting at the top when you're fresh out of high school, I thought. God and the Navy sure knew what they were doing. Well, at least God did!

But all of that was history. Where do I go from here? My next step? It's time to pray!

"Dear Lord, I must know Your will! If I ever needed divine guidance, now's the time! The doctor is waiting to hear from me. And I am waiting to hear from You. I praise You for the assurance that You will answer."

Since I knew that I could take my time for this important decision, I simply resolved that I would not let go of the altar of God until I was absolutely sure that my decision was based upon wisdom from above! Did not the book of James in the New Testament offer wisdom for the asking?[3]

I got my answer from God all right. But, it was not what I expected. At first it seemed impossible. Then...gradually...I came to realize that it all made good sense. His answer: **"Practice what you preached."**

As you might expect, I had been preaching from my youth that the Word of God, the Holy Bible, is chock-full of essential advice for businessmen and women. Now the shoe must go on the other foot. The businessman will be me!

What an advantage I will have over many, I thought. Many Scriptures raced through my mind. It seemed that the Holy Spirit brought these to me in rapid succession. It was an awesome experience! Then I simply thanked the Lord for the peace and assurance He gave me.

That I was to accept a medical separation from the Navy was made crystal clear. I gave the Navy my decision. Coincidentally, the day the Bureau of Naval Personnel picked for my separation was exactly eleven years from the day I reported for duty at the Naval Training Center in San Diego as a boot Lieutenant (jg) right out of seminary. To God be the glory! The pivotal day was 10 June 1971.

I've always had a fondness for numbers. Not mathematics per se, but the way numbers played a role in many of my experiences. Take the 3s, 7s and the 40s, for example. Some of my interest undoubtedly grew out of biblical studies.

I am keenly aware now that my life fell neatly into two twenty-one year segments: preaching for the first half and practicing for the second half...extending to the publication of this autobiography. Isn't that like half for God and half for self? you might ask. Not at all! Ministry and daily work in our chosen field must dovetail. While my disability might disqualify me for effective leadership, it would not hinder me from lay activites in a local church either. (There's something about the work of the Lord which permits handicappers of all kinds with a will to serve to get involved!) Also, didn't I preach that businessmen should not neglect church attendance? And didn't I preach the whole counsel of God, such as tithing, offerings, benevolence and humility?

The more I thought about the possibilities that were out there in my new future, the more excited I became. Just think of the rare chance which the Lord is giving me! It will certainly be a big change, to be sure. But the transition from pulpit to pew was going to be adventuresome, a joy, not troublesome! How did I know this? I knew it because I had heard from God. He was leading. My hearing loss embraced sound waves which were terrestrial only. I could still hear God's voice! We're talking "celestial!"

Optimistic by nature, I could hardly wait to get started. With God as my Partner, this whole venture will be one adventure after another! I'm under His control.

I was starting anew a bit late in life, admittedly. But look at the plus side. I felt as though I almost had to be careful not to take unfair advantage of business folk. Well, almost.

On the positive side, I had a solid education based upon God's eternal Word, excellent health (sans perfect hearing), plenty of ambition, and a loving, devoted wife.

I also owned an 8-unit apartment (St. Helens), some acreage in Graham and thirteen rental houses in Washington state. Those worldly goods and $31,000 severance pay hardly made me a millionaire, unless you count eternity. But I was hardly your basic candidate for pity either!

The title of this book requires an answer to at least two questions. What did he preach? And what did he practice? The answers give the book its two main parts. Between these main divisions are three chapters wherein preaching and practicing overlap into relevance and practicality.

Part One contains six chapters which, in a broad sense, fall into the category of PREACHING. The three chapters at the heart or middle of the book, chapters eight through ten, reveal the relevance and practicality of applying biblical principles to daily living. They appear in the first person as does this Introduction and the sixteenth chapter. With the exception of the first-person chapters cited above, the book was written in the third person simply because it seemed best for the reader's comfort and satisfaction.

Unless otherwise noted, the King James Version of the Bible was used. Other versions were abbreviated as NKJV for the New King James Version and TLB for The Living Bible.

The reader will encounter a few experiences in this book which overlap and will be found elsewhere in the book. This repetitious nature of the work was deemed somewhat beneficial rather than distracting. The late Dr. Kenneth Wesche, theology professor at Western Evangelical Seminary, observed wisely that "the price of everlasting possession is eternal repetition." I do hope you agree.

Chapter One, for example, includes some of the Vietnam story and the hospitalization since this chapter was written from a chronological approach. The same experiences appear in other chapters in more detail. This chapter presents an overview. That it speaks of adventure probably has more to do with what I wanted out of life. That it speaks of abundance undoubtedly has more to do with the kind of life Jesus promises to all who believe He is the Son of God.

Chapter Two tells how this book got its title. It also includes a glimpse of my preaching, some sermon outlines and a few titles with texts. I preached my heart out.

Chapter Three shows how I got started in the ministry: by starting a church for the deaf in the Ballard district of

Seattle. It tells about pioneering a church for the deaf also in Tacoma and of support under the Home Missions Department of the Assemblies of God in Springfield, Missouri.

Chapter Four is a fun chapter about a hilarious coincidence which came at an otherwise difficult period of transition in my life. The experience brought joy and hope. It came in a threeness.

Chapter Five deals with a cruise to the Far East and the opportunity for ministry aboard destroyers en route to the Western Pacific ports. I would not trade my experience aboard naval vessels at sea for all the tea in China. Yes, God is everywhere. But there is something about plowing through the ocean on a clear, moonlit night that brings one face to face with the awesome Creator of it all!

Chapter Six traces the action of the Third Marine Division in Vietnam and my assignments with combat troops of the U. S. Marines. You may be wondering what a Navy chaplain is doing in Vietnam with the Marines. The answer to that one is that the U. S. Marine Corps uses "Navy" chaplains, physicians, dentists and medical corpsmen, to name just a few in the support team. Incidentally, Navy chaplains may be assigned also to units of the U. S. Coast Guard. After two assignments in Vietnam, I volunteered for a third assignment.

Chapter Seven examines the preëminent position of praise in worship from the biblical view. It shows examples of the way praise not only fits into one's worship of God, but belongs also in our daily attitude toward life itself. A clarion call in the preaching of David, the Psalmist, and St. Paul, the Apostle, praise is enjoined in both Old and New Testaments.

Chapter Eight deals with what the elements of praise mean to me, with the styles of praise I prefer, and with what I found was effective to win and raise the spirits of men and women in military service. It shows the relevance of this great biblical emphasis in our moment-by-moment living as well as in the hour of corporate worship at church.

Chapter Nine is slanted toward youth, especially teenagers. But it will be helpful to college students. It contains some preaching — even a little meddling, with an aim toward practicality. Basic stuff. The way to an abundant life in Christ!

Chapter Ten demonstrates the fact that Northwest College of the Assemblies of God in Kirkland, Washington, played a significant role in my ministry. Both in the formative years of preparation and later in the administrative duties as Public Relations Director, Northwest College was the center of learning and experiencing. I will always carry fond memories of this great institution and its friendly faculty.

Part Two contains nine chapters which, in a broad sense, fall into the category of PRACTICING. The aim was to illustrate beyond the shadow of a doubt that applying biblical principles to the business world can lead to increasing levels of abundance, joy and success. I can only hope the reader will agree that while I tackled entrepreneurship my way, I did not lose sight of the urgency to do it His way.

Chapter Eleven begins the very worldly record of successes in the real estate market: buying, selling, leasing, managing and counseling. It reviews the reason for and the timing of a change in careers. It not only shows how it was possible to collect several income parcels, but points out a few by location. This chapter affords an overview of the "practicing" segment of the years which followed 1971. Father and son make a living the old fashioned way...by sowing and reaping.

Chapter Twelve graphically illustrates how God can take a small thing and make it a thing of joy and abundance. It shows how little can be much when God is in it! It also teaches, "If the shoe fits, wear it." But that lesson will be learned best...by reading the chapter.

Chapter Thirteen relates a joyous adventure with the acquisition, upgrading and sale of the ancient landmark in downtown Puyallup known as the St. Helens Apartments. It recounts a "slow miracle" where in ten years an investment of $1,444 cash and a little personal property resulted in an unexpected check for $105,750.00.

Chapter Fourteen is a brief faith-building account of an experience where a certain key was necessary to open an important door. The miraculous way that key appeared and its relevance to numerous other similar experiences one may encounter in life, makes this a fascinating true story. Good thing Donna was with me at the time to corroborate this one!

Chapter Fifteen tells about a memorable experience in the field of teaching which was unique and refreshing. I guess it illustrates the fact that a Christian believer can find joy in the most unlikely places...even in prison. Come to think of it, the Apostle Paul did!

Chapter Sixteen explains why I believe in faith promises. It also reveals the part that real estate contracts played in making good on a few faith promises and gives some practical ideas on how to collect and maintain them as investments.

Chapter Seventeen might very well be the most important chapter in this book. It relates a mountain-top experience which happened on a Holy Land tour in 1985. This marvelous encounter ties together for me both the baptism in the Holy Ghost and predestination. It shows how God can bring joy to our hearts by interposing events which, due to their timing, are beyond natural or human expectation. The subject matter dealt with in this chapter and climbing Mt. Sinai ranks among the most exhilarating events in my life. The inspiration drawn from that special day will stay with me as long as I live on planet earth. There's no earthly explanation for its timing!

Chapter Eighteen is all about a fine service club and my hometown in which it is located. To join this club when the invitation came was easy. For one thing, the "service to others" ideal is not unlike the teachings of Christ. Secondly, what better way to rub shoulders with men and women of the business community? I had advocated civic involvement in my preaching. Now I could practice what I preached. Besides, it's not drudgery. Being active in a Rotary Club can be an awfully lot of fun, even if you're not lucky enough to live in Puyallup, Washington.

Chapter Nineteen looks back on a good year in business. The story looks at the expectations of our silent partner, the Internal Revenue Service. Didn't we preach that we should not cheat? My generous contribution to IRS will show how I played by the rules. It's the only fair way for us to survive in America.

1

Adventure
and Abundance

"My purpose is to give life in all its fullness."
- Jesus in John 10:10b, The Living Bible

If anyone believed in God in the Richardson family, the secret was very well kept. Ronald got absolutely no encouragement from his father or mother to attend church, worship or read the Bible.

It was commonly accepted that when Olive Pauline Packard married Ned National Richardson, she may have landed one of the handsomest of the nine sons of Charles and Minnie Richardson, but he was also the braggart of all the boys. Nellie was the only girl.

As it turned out, Ronald did not accept the Lord as his Savior until he was a high school sophomore. The matter simply had not been brought to his attention before that.

A logger mostly, Ned worked hard enough, but wasn't able to put away anything for a rainy day. In later years Ned learned the shoe repair business and opened shoe shops in

1

Olympia, Puyallup, Centralia and Portland, Oregon. He became an industrious entrepreneur with adequate income.

Ron's mother was twenty and Ned twenty-two when Ronald arrived in September 1928. Three years and two months later, Donald Dean introduced himself to the family. That was it...all there would be...two boys for Ned and Olive.

Poverty was everywhere in those depression days. Ron didn't notice it much, or even cared. Life itself was the big thing and there were always lots of exciting things to do. Hunting frogs was one of them! The family lived in a small cabin on the east bank of the Carbon River in Orting, Washington. Frogs were just a hobby, so don't jump to conclusions! There was little money to be had in raising them. Wild huckleberries and wild strawberries were all over the hillside. Salmon were plentiful upstream for the gaffing. Deer were out there and Ned got his share for the family table.

But times were hard. The foot bridge washed out over the Carbon River and Ronnie carried Dean piggy back, crossing the knee-deep river to reach the south side to attend Orting Elementary public school. Dean's shoes were barely sturdy enough to protect the tender feet of a second-grader.

Ronnie (as Dean called his older brother) was a sixth-grader at the Orting school. His favorite teacher, Mrs. McGee, taught the parts of speech by rote memory definitions. A half century later, Ron recalled that "an adverb is a word that modifies a verb, adjective or another adverb, and answers the questions how, when, where, or to what degree?" and that "A preposition is a word that introduces a phrase and shows relation between the principal word in the phrase and some other word in the sentence."

Too short to make much of a mark in sports, Ronald did turn out for track. He did best in the fifty yard dash, but that was only because his hearing was keen and he got off to a good start. How he wished he had the long legs of the sixth grade's star runner, Ernie Lemka! No one for miles around in any of the schools could come close to beating Ernie on the track.

Olive found work as a waitress, a job that she learned to enjoy. She stuck with it her whole life through. Known best

2

among waitresses by the nickname "Sally," the cute, dark-haired charmer held positions in a few of the finer restaurants in Tacoma and Puyallup. For many years, Olive waited table at Nettie's Cafe in Puyallup. She was also in charge of hiring enough waitresses to serve at the Western Washington Fair's Nettie's Farmhouse.

For a time, the two boys lived with their grandparents in Olympia. Olive's father and brother were barbers in an Olympia shop. It was such fun for the boys to visit the shop. The old grandfather clock ticked away the seconds. The smell of the lotions. It was all a pleasant visit except for the haircuts. It didn't seem to matter how still Ron and Dean sat on the board across the chair arms, those old hand clippers never failed to pull hair!

Nonetheless, it was a good thing Ron knew where that barber shop was located. A school bus ride on his first day of school in the first grade drew a blank! One by one the kids got off the bus, but Ron could not recognize the place to get off.

"Where do you live, son?" the driver asked.

"I don't know," Ron replied, "But grandpa's shop is on 4th Avenue!"

Few teenagers can sit down and plan their vocation and know the education required, then stick to that plan to the end. Life simply does not go along without hitches!

And Ron did not plan to be a chaplain aboard destroyers or to serve with combat troops in Vietnam. But that is the way the Lord led!

Finding the Lord Jesus Christ as his personal Savior at age 16, he made it a regular habit to go to the prayer tower in the Olympia Foursquare Church and wait upon the Lord. On the way to high school this was the stop that made the day go right. While there, he read Scripture and prayed. He took literally the promise in Jeremiah 33:3 which states:

"Call unto me, and I will answer thee, and shew thee great and mighty things, which thou knowest not."

Although he did not receive an audible answer as he had thought he might, his ministerial career would one day show

3

him great and mighty things. Nevertheless, that career was not to be for an entire lifetime. It would be cut short. Still, the abrupt change in the course of his life by no means ended his ministry. He would learn first-hand the very thing he used to preach — namely, that laymen can be ministers, too! So Ron was to reach a point in his life, at age 43, when he would face a crisis — at least in his vocational pursuit. As explained in more detail in this book, God told him to practice in business what he used to preach in pulpits.

And from that day in June of 1971 down to the present in so-called "retirement," Ron continues following the "second commission."

Ron was short. You would not guess him to be his 5' 6" unless he stood up straight! "I look up to everybody," he would often say. What he lacked in stature, he compensated for in energy, determination and persistence.

As a businessman, Ron discovered early that those years of study in the Word gave him an edge. The teachings of Jesus Christ were applicable to all facets of life. He gave God the glory, attributing all business success to the manifestation of well-known biblical principles.

His life was a merger of two widely divergent fields: theology and real estate. His life is a tale of an unlikely marriage of the two! Just as some eggs have two yolks, his life brought together two dreams: the ministry (as a pastor and navy chaplain) and real estate (as a broker, property manager and investor).

Ron's biography is unique because it shows the value of determination and planning for a career in life. But it also shows how faith and patience can pave the way for a transition from one career to another. What makes his story uncommon is the way he dealt with a physical impairment which demanded a change in careers in mid-life.

After a lengthy series of tests in two naval hospitals, DeBock decided to leave active naval service and to **"practice what he preached"** from pulpits and counseling on land and sea, civilian and military for about 21 years. It all began when he accepted Christ as his Lord and Savior as a teenager.

4

Accepts Christ

The real beginning for a fuller life was when Ron accepted Christ at age 16. He was living with his grandparents in Olympia at the time. That they were less than enthusiastic concerning his involvement at the church would be putting it mildly. At mealtime while he would bow to say grace, his grandmother would rattle the pans loudly on the cooking stove. He overheard her tell his grandfather, "Ronald has gotten religion, but he'll outgrow it." As it turned out, he had not outgrown it seven years later when he would conduct his first funeral at the request of the family. Lena Packard, his grandmother, was 75.

One Sunday morning Ron was walking by the Foursquare Church in Olympia. John Dotson, a congenial deacon, invited the boy to join him for a morning worship service. He did, and that was the beginning of a growing relationship. "Brother Dotson" was a godly father figure to Ron at a crucial time in his life. In fact, the broken home was the reason he was staying with his grandparents during this period of time.

After attending the Sunday School and worship services for a few weeks, Ron went to an evening service. It was less formal than the morning services. That night Pastor Roy Mourer preached from John 3:16-18. He accepted Christ with tears. The meeting lasted so long that he missed the last bus home. But that was no problem. He ran the entire two miles home, singing and praising the Lord all the way, mostly up hill. A big load had been lifted. Ronald was a new young man in Christ Jesus!

A quiet, serious student, Ron began studying the Bible diligently. He especially wanted to learn more about the Christian life and to grow in the understanding of this new walk of faith. He was baptized in water and had his heart set on receiving the Holy Spirit. (This experience would not take place until many weeks later...on March 13, 1945, in the Shelton Foursquare Church at a mid-week prayer meeting).

Lots of faith...but no money!

Wanting desperately to go to college, but having no money

for tuition, Ron made the matter one of constant prayer, at the old-fashioned altar in the prayer room at Puyallup First Assembly. (He drove to Puyallup for high school and church from Tacoma where he was living with his mother and stepfather, the late Gustaf DeBock).

The Lord told Ron to join the Navy. He did as he was told, with the Navy granting him ten days leave in which to graduate from high school, after being sworn in.

Following six weeks of boot camp at San Diego, his first and only assignment was as a yeoman striker at the Bureau of Naval Personnel in Washington, D. C. He spent most of the two years in the Officer Promotions Section as a commander's secretary, which included typing bills for Congress.

A little romance blossomed

Ron met Donna June Walsworth at the Puyallup church. The shy country girl really knew her Bible, committing much of it to memory!

The church conducted a Scripture Memory contest in which Donna and Ron were contestants. It was the first time the two had met as Ron was new to the church. Both had committed several chapters to memory. They look back with nostalgia on that match because it led to a lasting matchup a few years later. Courtship followed the competition. In that sense, both of them were winners! Donna was always favored to win such contests. But this time she placed second. The new boy in church carried a large black Bible with well-worn pages.

Hard Work and the G. I. Bill

Ron longed to go to college. Following two years' active duty in the Navy, he could use earned benefits under the G. I. Bill. Subsistence was more for married veterans. He thought much about that possibility, too. All matters were weighed carefully and prayerfully.

He enrolled in a pre-Med course at the College of Puget Sound in Tacoma in the fall of 1948 under his new name, Ronald DeBock. He changed his name from Richardson to

DeBock by means of a Court Order in March of that year. He opted for the ministry and enrolled in Northwest Bible College in September of 1949. Donna and Ron said their marriage vows in the same month. Now life was really taking on new excitement!

Ron took a full load of studies and worked part time to support his family. He worked in a candy factory, as an orderly in a tuberculosis sanatorium, as a process server for a group of attorneys, and as a salesman for a real estate firm. He enjoyed selling homes and soon was made sales manager at Northgate Brokers in Seattle.

God says "NO," too!

During his senior year at Northwest Bible College, Ron lived in a cozy one-bedroom house in Lake City. He had an option to buy the home. It was situated on a fenced half-acre, loaded with rhododendrons nestled under tall evergreen trees. A year 'round creek meandered along one side of the property. Gleaming white bookshelves flanked a colorful brick fireplace. Ron thought it was time to be specific in prayer. "Lord, I'd like to own this particular house. What must I do to help you answer this prayer?"

He got an answer all right. But it was not what he hoped for. However, the answer was one the young minister would never forget! "My son, seek my will, obey me, and houses will gather to you." As for the Lake City house, the answer was NO!

The very next day a call came from Reverend Ralph Phillips, then the Secretary-Treasurer of the Northwest District Council of the Assemblies of God. He asked Ron if he would be interested in an interim pastorate at the Montesano Assembly of God. He gladly responded affirmatively! When Ron and Donna discovered the church had just built a new three-bedroom parsonage, they were surprised. Was this how God was answering their prayer? Perhaps, a little foretaste. The best was yet to come! Ron thought, "Even God's NOs might include something POSITIVE with it!" Reader, are you willing to wait years...many years...for an answer to your prayer?

7

Seven years of pastoral ministry

Montesano was DeBock's first full-time pastorate. His pastorates in Washington state were in Montesano, Mineral, Lakebay and Longbranch. The latter two were community churches only four miles apart on the lower Olympic Peninsula.

Move On!

During the springtime of 1957, Ron began to dream of new horizons. He thought of his Navy days following high school, and of the great opportunities for ministry to men in uniform. He had also received some significant encouragement from Reverend Douglas Scott, then Executive Director of the National Association of Evangelicals. It was time to make this possible change of directions a matter of prayer!

Back to the books!

"Get ready to move," God said, "It will be hard, but I will give you strength to the end!" So DeBock, his wife, Donna, and their three children, moved into a small house on the campus of Western Evangelical Seminary in Portland, Oregon. Ron entered in September, 1957, receiving also a commission in the U. S. Naval Reserve as an "ensign probationary" the same month. On receiving word of the commission, he picked up his little daughter, Beverly, and danced all around the house, singing and praising the Lord. (There can be no greater satisfaction than seeing God work out His plan in your life!)

The probationary commission had an interesting twist for Ron. The seminary had accepted him into a Greek course "on probation" since he lacked the prerequisite course. At the same time, he landed a job with the Portland post office which placed all new employees in a probationary status for their first year. Thus, he found himself "on probation" in three arenas simultaneously, a humbling position indeed!

Raising a family, studying, and working (all at the same time) can be a tough road. But hadn't God promised strength? Ron stayed with it, received high marks and graduated in

May, 1960, with a Master of Divinity degree.

A letter from the Navy Chief of Chaplains arrived three months before graduation, advising Ensign DeBock that orders to active duty awaited his graduation and that his first assignment would be at the U. S. Naval Training Center in San Diego.

Chaplain DeBock became an effective evangelical minister to men and women in uniform. His assignments included Destroyer Division 232, home ported at Long Beach, California (1961-63) and at the Naval Air Station, Memphis, Tennessee (1963-64). He then donned a Marine Corps uniform and was assigned to the 3rd Marine Regiment on Okinawa, in 1964. When the war escalated in Vietnam, he left for Da Nang in June of 1965, where he served with Marine troops. He would be awarded three Vietnam service medals.

Interest in Japanese Culture and Language

As a boy of 10, Ron picked strawberries and raspberries in fields in Puyallup Valley, owned by Japanese farmers. He watched Japanese children, admiring their competitive spirit. But Ron was competitive, too. And to show it, one morning he arrived to pick raspberries at 3:15 a.m., complete with flashlight in hand to assist the moonlight. He had nearly a flat picked before the Japanese kids got to the field! That was the day he began learning the Japanese language. They taught him how to count.

But DeBock did not begin to study Japanese seriously until shortly before a Western Pacific cruise. He knew that on the cruise in the Far East the ships would make many ports of call in Japan, and he wanted to be prepared.

Later, while stationed in Seattle at the Naval Supply Depot, he studied Japanese language at the University of Washington. The studies paid off handsomely as he received orders from there to serve as the Senior Chaplain at the Marine Corps Air Station in Iwakuni, Japan. The city is in Southern Honshu near Hiroshima.

Soon after arriving at Iwakuni, Ron began teaching elementary Japanese to military personnel and dependents. But he had a big surprise awaiting him. His son, Gary, was a high school sophomore at Iwakuni. It would not be long before Gary demonstrated a greater proficiency in the language than his father, who had been studying it for years!

The reader should know at this point that Ron had the breaks, but Gary had the brains!

With the G. I. Bill, good timing and financial backing, Ron was able to accumulate college credits and earn four academic degrees, including a Ph.D. But Gary had to change high schools every year, because of his dad's frequent moves during active naval service. However, Gary never took a test that he failed! He went through high schools with top grades, graduating from North Chicago High School second in a class of 217 seniors. He picked up the Japanese language rapidly, later studying it at the University of Hawaii.

Among Ron's collateral assignments at Iwakuni, the Orphanage Coordinator (for 13 nearby orphanages) was one of the more enjoyable ones. The Marines generously supported the kids, and the so-called "People to People" program was excellent public relations for the United States. A Marine pilot with the Air Wing quipped, "If this (orphanage) program gets any better, every orphan will be riding his own Honda!" The truth is that sweaters and softball equipment were more typical of the gifts procured for those orphans.

Frugality, the wisest investment

The DeBocks were thrifty to a fault. They never forgot the lean times. Their uncommonly frugal life-style permitted cash reserves for investment. Soon a pattern emerged. Nearly every time he got new orders, it meant it was time to add another rental house to the portfolio. Of course, this did prove to be taxing in more ways than one!

Ron found plenty of divine guidance from the Bible, when it came to realty investments. He employed the same faith in these endeavors as he did in other areas of ministry. Sometimes, he went out on a limb — but it never broke under him!

For example, he had the insignia of the next higher rank

sewn on his uniform **before each promotion** was made public. Similarly, he ordered five sets of furniture from an Okinawan manufacturer, to furnish a 7-unit apartment building (St. Helens) **before his offer to buy it was accepted** by the seller.

Vietnam again!

After two years at Iwakuni with his family, DeBock knew the picnic was over. It was back to Vietnam! Again, he was assigned to the Third Marine Division. This time the chaplain was assigned to a headquarters battalion near the DMZ (Demilitarized Zone).

This was no "police action," as some called it. This was war, and every Marine knew it! Back home in the States, the debate continued over whether America even belonged in the action.

The men appreciated their chaplains. They needed God at times like these! The chaplains pointed them to God. A few, who seldom attended a chapel back on Okinawa, made a habit of worship while in the combat zone. Whoever said, "There are no atheists in foxholes" could tell you why.

Chaplain DeBock felt needed, too. He keenly sensed that he was doing the very thing God wanted him to do and that all of the preparation leading up to this must be brought to bear upon those critical days with the fearful, the wounded and sometimes worse. He volunteered for a third tour in Vietnam on his duty preference sheet.

Remarkably, after a brief period of duty on Okinawa, he got his wish and returned to Vietnam for a third tour (1969-70). However, he grew restless and gradually became disenchanted with the futility of it all, and the lack of military progress. Of course, Ron knew he was there for **the ministry** — not to take lives. This was a big difference!

Three "Gary"s in Twelve?

About 12 men in battle gear headed for the front lines with Lima Company paused for a moment, while Chaplain DeBock had prayer with the squad. He took the time to hear

11

their first names before the send-off prayer. Of the squad, three were named "Gary." He felt a strong tie to these who were facing uncertainty at the front. And now, three of them have the same name as his 16-year-old son back home! More of this experience is in Chapter Six.

God can bring glory out of injury!

Shortly after reporting to Great Lakes, Illinois, Ron asked a medical officer to examine his ears and his hearing. This he did because he had been around some rather loud bursts while assigned to Marine Corps units on Okinawa and in Vietnam. A routine check-up seemed wise. But that *routine* check-up led to sixty-one consecutive days hospitalized, first at the Great Lakes Naval Hospital and then at the Naval Hospital in Philadelphia.

It was time to look back. Time to look ahead. Time to pray! He thought, "How easy to learn the will of God in this case. All I need to do is wait for the doctor's decision." There could be only two possible answers: (1) continued active duty, or (2) medical separation. Which would it be?

Advice came from all corners! Most of the voices said, "Stay in the Navy!" But some said, "Get out!" A lot was at stake! Thirteen active military years had been logged in (two as a "white hat" and eleven as a chaplain).

While an in-patient at the Philadelphia Naval Hospital, a letter arrived from the Bureau of Naval Personnel advising Ron that his temporary rank had been changed to the permanent grade of lieutenant commander.

The medical officer finally gave the verdict — that is, the evaluation and report of the medical board. "Well, yours is a borderline case," he began. "You may either remain on active duty or be medically discharged. The decision is yours."

What the good doctor did not know was that God had already been preparing him for this moment — yet the decision would be the hardest one of his life!

When at the Crossroads, go to Prayer!

The Navy was not in a hurry for a decision. It was "Take

your time. Take a week or two. Think it over and let us know your decision." Chaplain DeBock wanted a clear word from God! He had learned long ago that, when one is at the crossroads, it is time to go to prayer! God had not failed him in the past to point the way. After all, "the steps of a good man are ordered by the Lord: and He delighteth in his way." (Psalms 37:23) KJV.

So Ron went again to the small chapel in the hospital for prayer. He wanted an unmistakable signal and there was not a doubt in his mind that God was about to speak. (Incidentally, He always speaks when we listen!). Finally, God spoke in a clear voice....

Practice What You Preached!

"Now practice what you preached," God said. That was it. That was the answer he was waiting for! Return to civilian life. To do what, though? That was still an unknown. Retirement? No, he was too young for that! Besides, Ron believed that retirement is more an attitude than anything. And just because he could not hear high-pitched tones or distinguish softly spoken words, that did not mean he should be put on the shelf! Now, it seems that he must carefully put into practice all those Golden Rule ideas he had preached about from pulpits in civilian churches, military chapels and shipboard messdecks for more than twenty years, as an active minister of the Gospel of Christ.

"Practice what you preached!" Those words came again and again to Ron's thoughts as he prayed. At first he took them to be his own conscience, exhorting him to be earnest in prayer. He had urged servicemen to pray in faith, now he was urging the same good counsel upon himself. He had often turned to the promises in the Bible concerning divine guidance, fervently preaching that the Lord is personally mindful of every step His children take! "God really cares for you," was a reoccurring theme in Ron's pulpit ministry. But when he renewed his pleading for guidance, and the same emphatic phrase returned again, he suddenly recognized it for God's voice. What **had** he been preaching?

13

So Chaplain DeBock asked for and received orders separating him from active duty on June 10, 1971, exactly eleven years from the day he entered active duty as a chaplain. He had served five of those years with the U. S. Marine Corps. A 43-year old man in excellent health except for a hearing loss, returned to his hometown, Puyallup, Washington, to prayerfully await his next orders. They would not be from the Chief of Navy Chaplains, but from his Commander-in-Chief, the very God of the Universe! Now it was no longer Chaplain DeBock, but Mr. R. G. DeBock.

Watch out, you civilians!

President D. V. Hurst of Northwest College called just days after Ron had settled into his home in Puyallup. The call was an invitation to join the college's staff as the Director of Public Relations. "I'd like to think about it and pray about it first," Ron replied. There was a pause... "I've thought about it and prayed about it, and would like to come to Kirkland to your office and talk about it next week." He remained at the college for 3 $1/_2$ years. During this time the student enrollment enjoyed at least 13 quarters of continuous increases. (Student recruitment was a primary responsibility of the position.) This by no means implies that the PR Director deserves the credit! Far from it! But it was encouraging to witness the steady growth of the enrollment during those years (1972-75).

Since the DeBocks had averaged the purchase of at least one rental house per year while on active military duty, absentee management of these properties posed only a little problem for them while in Kirkland. Gradually, however, a new and significant *ministry* began to emerge. Missionaries and other clergymen began to knock on Ron's door because here was one of their own with experience in the technical field of rental house management. A minister must go overseas for a four year assignment, for example. What will he do with the house? The word got around. Why not let Ron DeBock handle it while the missionary is away from the mainland?

Requests for management services increased. Not only did he manage properties for his friends, but he acquired a few rental houses for his own growing portfolio.

After three and one-half years, DeBock resigned his position at the college. It was not an easy decision, because he enjoyed the PR job and the good fellowship with faculty, students and area ministers. But it was time to leave and he knew it.

God's Assignments are for a Time Frame

While showing off the beautiful campus to some prospective students one day, DeBock heard God's voice. "Move to the center of Puyallup. I will show you the place."

It was important for Ron that he maintain good faith with the administration at Northwest College. It was agreed that he would remain at the college until a replacement was named.

He bought an old two-story house with ten rooms and two full baths in the middle of Puyallup. A new business was born called **"Rainier Rentals."**

It was destined to grow like a tree, reminding Ron of the tree in the first Psalm.

If you think education is expensive, try ignorance!

In the technical field of real estate management, education would be important. DeBock entered Tacoma Community College, completing a two-year real estate course with an Associate in Arts degree. At the same time, he was in a doctoral program to build on the Master of Divinity degree he had already earned.

With his marching orders in hand, Ron felt that God was leading. He prayerfully studied.[5]

The challenge was somehow to bring theology and real estate together as he racked his brain for some common ground. At first, these two fields seemed miles apart! Would it be possible? How could it be done? Perhaps a better question might be, "Why should it be attempted?"

To undertake a study of parsonages didn't make any sense since these had become less popular with the clergy due to the more favorable benefits of home ownership with housing allowances from the church.

Finally, DeBock decided to write a doctoral dissertation about where the money came from to build new churches. Real estate finance! The dissertation was entitled **"A Comparison Between the Financing of New Worship Facilities of the Assemblies of God and Nazarenes in Washington State."**

When the fog lifted, Ron had earned two academic degrees in early 1979, the Associate of Arts in Real Estate from Tacoma Community College, and a Doctor of Philosophy from the California Graduate School of Theology. His latest studies rounded out ten years of classroom work beyond high school.

One little seed...and God!

Practicing what he used to preach meant diligence, patience and much perseverance. It also meant hard work! But doors soon opened. For one semester, the new "Dr." DeBock taught a course in Real Estate for Tacoma Community College.

Meanwhile, Rainier Rentals continued to grow. On the first day of business, October 7, 1975, one phone call in the morning and a $5 fee that afternoon told the day's activity. Now that's a small beginning! Yet, Ron wrote in his diary, "It is only a whisper of a start, but I'm encouraged!"

Like a tree starting from a seed planted on the corner of Fifth and West Main, the little property management business grew until it became one of Puyallup's most remarkable success stories. The firm became popular with large and small investors. Ron was nicknamed "The Renter's Chaplain." He recalled, too, how he wanted to buy that little home in Lake City 23 years earlier, but could not get an OK from his heavenly Father. It took that long for him to understand the answer God gave him to that prayer request! Reader, have you prayed and wondered about the strange answer you have received? Perhaps, God has something more wonderful waiting for you than you dare to believe now!

By 1985, the firm managed some 289 units, two-thirds of which were single family homes. The firm's annual gross rents reached $1.4 million and Rainier Rentals was only ten years old.

Who were the owners of these rental units? Of course, they came from all walks of life. Many were local owners and others from out of state. Some were professional men and women such as doctors, lawyers, pilots and career military personnel. Not only were they individuals, but institutions with homes to manage. A bank in Seattle, a university in California, a college in Washington state. Where did the universities get the houses? They were often donated by members of the Alumni Association or by friends of the institutions.

Retirement is merely an attitude.

The fact that Ron was nearing the age when many think of retirement was of little consequence. He enjoyed good health and felt that the word "retirement" had little meaning for him. It was just an attitude or a state of mind. He did not think that age 43 was old enough to stop dreaming or to stop the great exhilaration of living. It was an adventure he enjoyed! That dreams become a reality has been proven by many in America. But, the drive that pushed him forward was undoubtedly the sincere belief in the "abundant life" promises of his Savior and Lord Jesus Christ.[6]

Ron dreamed once and became a chaplain in the Navy. He dreamed again, and became manager of rental properties for others. When interest rates soared to double digit levels in 1980, his firm surged ahead. None of this happened by accident. It was all in God's hands. When it came to management of residential properties, DeBock had prepared himself, Moreover, his penchant for an ultra-conservative bank posture led to the rule-of-thumb level of less than one-to-eight debt-to-assets ratio. Growth charts revealed a 42 percent annual growth in personal net worth for the decade following his separation from active naval service in 1971.

In December, 1985, Ron and Donna bought a lovely antique style two-story home near the rental office. This permitted expansion of the office which was previously used for living quarters.

In October, 1992, he made substantial improvements on

the business location. This work included remodelling of an overhead apartment, a new exterior porch and landscaping.

As he was putting the finishing touches on this book, Ron was working on plans for a 40th Anniversary of Ordination celebration (April, 1993). His son, Gary, was enjoying duties as manager of the business, and helping Ruth, his young bride, learn English in preparation for the nursing profession.

His daughter, Beverly, along with her husband, Frank Satter, was busy caring for Ron and Donna's two lovely grand-daughters, Angela and Ashley. How convenient that these sweet little girls live in nearby Graham! Grandma and Grandpa get to see them once or twice a week! The bumper stickers are right: *Happiness is being a grandparent.*

Ned National Richardson
(Ron's father at age 21)

2

What Did He Preach?

"...I solemnly urge you before God and before Christ Jesus...
to preach the Word of God...whenever you get the chance, in season
and out, when it is convenient and when it is not...encourage them to
do right, and all the time be feeding them patiently with God's Word."
- 2 Timothy 4:1-2, TLB

Why don't you **"practice what you preach?"**

Have you ever heard that idiom-like expression? An-other phrase which is similar in meaning is: "Your actions speak so loudly that I can't hear what you are saying." Both expressions seek a non-hypocritical life-style with right living as opposed to mere words, without evidence of good works.

When Ron DeBock heard from God, "Practice what you preached," an accumulation of no less than twenty-one years of pulpit work had to be collated. Yet, this would not be a formidable task, since he had carefully kept a record of every sermon title, text, date preached, and location in a pastoral record book, along with the data concerning 78 weddings and 76 funerals.

Understandably, Ron asked himself, "What have I preached?" (It's a good question for any minister to ask himself, incidentally!) At this particular juncture for Ron, though, he felt a two-fold need to assess 21 years of preaching. First, due to his choice of real estate as his next career, his **preaching days** might be, for all practical purposes, concluded. Secondly, in the light of the answer God gave him to his prayer for wisdom, (in June of 1971 at the Philadelphia Naval Hospital), his second career was to be guided uniquely **by godly advice from his own tongue!**

Isn't life interesting?! As a child in elementary school, we watch other children intently. There is good reason for this, of course. If we show a behavior pattern much like the majority of other children, it follows that we are quite normal as a young human being. Then comes junior high and high school. We continue to observe our contemporaries carefully, with a view to seeing ourselves better. How do we fit in the scheme of it all?

This habit does not end with graduation from high school or college, either. On and on it goes. Perhaps, it never ends. There is evidence in all walks of life that we take comfort in equalling or bettering our contemporaries in achievements, dubiously measured by grade levels, commendations, pay scales or position titles.

The military is a good example. DeBock noted that it became easier and easier to tell which "boots" had been in boot camp the longest. Since in his company at the Recruit Training Command, San Diego, all young men got the same haircut, that made the job easier. Just look at the length of their hair! At least, this was a better clue than judging by the way they marched on the grinder! After just a few months' active duty, **the uniform** a person wore revealed just about all you wanted to know about the sailor, but were afraid to ask.

Through all of his life until age 43, DeBock had little difficulty in observing his contemporaries. All he had to do was look at the roster of chaplains within his own denomination, the Assemblies of God, to know who they were, which part of America they came from, their rank and branch of military service. Pastors would be listed alphabetically in a volume published annually by the church, known as the Offi-

<u>cial</u> <u>List</u> of <u>Ministers</u>.

But, no longer! No more contemporaries! Show me one other former navy chaplain with thirteen active duty years of military service who has been given a medical separation for a cause (hearing loss) severe enough to prevent him from fulfilling his ministerial calling, yet not severe enough to keep him from seeking a selected second career. DeBock thought along those lines. "From now on, buddy, you're on your own," he reasoned. Except that he knew better. For God had said, "I will never leave thee, nor forsake thee." (Hebrews 13:5) And God also said, "In all thy ways acknowledge Him, and He shall direct thy paths." (Proverbs 3:6)

Yes, Ron DeBock knew the biblical promises well. Furthermore, he had that personal word from the Lord as a result of praying for wisdom... **"Practice what you preached!"** Where are his contemporaries who had been given an orbital change of course at about mid-point along the celestial path from earth to glory? He was alone with his thoughts: "Stand up now and make yourself known, all ye who have come to a mid-life crisis! Let us not give up. Let's make the best of it. Let's move forward...in the name of Jesus...let's march on in victory. God will lead the way, I know it! Take His hand and He'll lead you. Follow me, let's go!"

If it's in the Bible, chances are good that he preached it. Yes, it's such a marvelous Bible and uniquely speaks to every human problem. The Word of God certainly deals with all essential matters.

If it isn't in the Bible, it doesn't belong in the pulpit. He strived to make his messages practical. He believed and preached that the fruit of the Spirit should be **visible:** love, joy, peace...and all!

From the Word of God, the Holy Bible, Ron believed it taught that:

(1) A person should be thankful for everything that comes his way, and learn to rejoice in adversity.

(2) A person should strive to be fair with others.

(3) Love is a strong motivation and should be preeminent.

(4) You cannot love others unless you love yourself first.
(5) Hard work is a lost art. It pays great dividends!
(6) Sowing and reaping is as reliable as gravity.
(7) God does not withhold good things from the deserving.
(8) When you can't understand, it's time to trust God!
(9) There is a thirst which only Jesus can quench.
(10) God made us like Himself. So, let's be creative!
(11) Little things can be big...if you add the Creator.
(12) There's probably a better way than your last effort.
(13) Anyone who really seeks God will surely find Him!
(14) Three places to look for God are in the sky, in the Bible and in the heart. (See Psalm 19)
(15) The best way to start is by using what you have on hand.

Some of Ron's favorite sermon titles (with biblical texts) were:

(1) Numbered Hairs ....Matt. 10:30
(2) The Water Jesus Gives ....Isa. 12:3
(3) A Matter of Life and Death.........................Heb. 9:27
(4) Reverencing God's Voice.............................Rev. 3:20
(5) Three Places to Find God............................Psalm 19
(6) The Popularity of Christ ....Mk. 12:37
(7) Peace, Be Still..Mk. 4:39
(8) Sower, Seed, Soil ....Matt. 13
(9) It's the Water! ....John 4
(10) But if Not! ....Dan. 3:18
(11) Thanksgiving & Victory ....I Thess. 5:16
(12) Come unto Me ....Matt. 11:28
(13) When God Laughs..Psalm 2:4
(14) The Man in the Middle ....Matt. 27:38
(15) Let God Talk, Too ....Jer. 33:3
(16) Come and See ....Jn. 1:46
(17) Flickering Lamps...Matt. 25:6
(18) Twenty/Twenty Vision ....Acts 20:20
(19) The Magnetic Christ ....Lk. 23:4
(20) Then Jesus Came ....Jn. 19:5
(21) A Call to Praise ....Ps. 107:8

Some of his own advice to parishioners, which Ron would do well to heed while working in his new business career might include the following:

(1) Do not neglect church attendance.

(2) Make Bible reading a regular habit.

(3) Walk with your head high, as a child of God!

(4) Don't forget that God is always nearby.

(5) Do not borrow more than you can quickly repay. Even better if you do not have to borrow!

(6) Keep in good health by not smoking, by eating right, and by getting plenty of exercise. Don't experiment with drugs!

(7) Never trust in your money alone. Trust in God!

(8) Do your work with all your might. Give it your best!

(9) Practice the "golden rule." It came from the lips of Jesus!

(10) Do not take a partner who is an unbeliever. Even better if you don't take any partner at all! Except your Friend.

(11) Be loyal to your employees, and expect loyalty in return.

(12) Treat all persons with fairness and equity. They are all God's children, and are deserving of respect. Remember, however, respect is not something you should expect. It must be earned!

(13) Forget about laying blame on others. You are the one who is responsible!

(14) Forgive always. Remember, God is the avenger — not you!

(15) Encourage yourself in the use of your best talents.

(16) Lay up for yourself **treasures in heaven.**

(17) Pray as though it all depends upon God. Work as though it all depends upon you!

(18) Being at a disadvantage can be an advantage...if you look up!

3

Ministry
to the Deaf

"So then faith cometh by hearing,
and hearing by the word of God."
- Romans 10:17

While stationed in Washington, D. C., Navy Seaman Ronald Richardson (name change to **DeBock** was not until 1948) became fascinated with sign language. The teenager who would one day be commissioned a Navy chaplain preferred to attend a civilian church on Massachusetts Avenue in the nation's capital, where the late Reverend Ben Mahan was pastor of The Full Gospel Tabernacle.

A warm and friendly couple attended that church, Paul and Coila Soules. He was an army pilot on active duty. She was deaf. But Coila was very good at projecting her voice and making herself understood!

Ron was eager to learn the sign language. He became more and more interested as he watched Coila interpret Pastor Mahan's sermons for deaf young people. He studied from a manual of signs. The seaman had no car, so he rode the bus

25

and practiced signing the poster ads which were always plastered throughout the bus. Young people from nearby Gallaudet College for the Deaf also attended that church. Ron became friends with them and learned their language.

Navy life need not be boring! Be open to what lies in front of you. This was fun! It took approximately fifteen months for Ron to advance to the level of communication skills which would enable him to present a Bible lesson in the American sign language.

Coila Soules was especially adept at teaching signs used in the language of the church. She not only taught Ron but anyone else who might show an interest. This was her ministry! For example, a star pupil was Lottie L. Riekehof, who would go on to further study of sign language, to teach and write reference books on the subject. Lottie became the very best at it!

It was not until Ron turned 21 that his fascination for the sign language would spell ministry. The story was described by E. J. Mitchell in the Seattle Post Intelligencer:

SIGN LANGUAGE FOR THE PULPIT
Student Minister Plans Series for the Deaf

A Seattle youth who taught himself the sign language because "it fascinated me" is going to use that talent to launch his preaching career.

Ronald G. DeBock, an Assemblies of God student minister, will begin regular church services for the deaf at 11 a.m. Sunday in the lower chapel of The Philadelphia Church at 6543 Jones Ave. N. W.

The new congregation, which now has about 12 members, is interdenominational, organized as the Christian Deaf Fellowship.

DeBock, 21, studied the sign language through books while he served as seaman first class in the Bureau of Naval Personnel in Washington, D. C. for two years.

He gained valuable help from several students of the Gallaudet College for the Deaf in Washington,

D. C., and practical experience as an interpreter for the deaf in several services at the Full Gospel Tabernacle in Washington in 1947.

"Whenever I saw persons talking with their hands I was really fascinated," he said Friday. "So I took up the sign language, merely as a hobby, but soon spent all my time studying it. And chumming around with some of the fellows from the college gave me the opportunity of 'talking' in the deaf language."

DeBock, a former student of the College of Puget Sound, Tacoma, and the Northwest Bible College, Seattle, hopes to make deaf preaching his ministerial career.

Ron married his childhood sweetheart, Donna Walsworth, at the start of his first year of study at Northwest Bible College. With his studies, the new deaf church, and finding enough income to support a wife and (later) children, the young ministerial student kept very busy.

Ministry to the deaf afforded opportunity for DeBock to obtain a license to preach earlier than Bible students without a special ministry. He not only held services for the deaf in Seattle, but began conducting worship services for the deaf in Tacoma in March of 1951. At first they were known as Christian Deaf Fellowship. Later they were Seattle Deaf Assembly and Tacoma Deaf Assembly.

For nearly 3 $^1/_2$ years, Reverend DeBock, his wife, Donna, along with a new baby daughter, Beverly, would make the trip each Sunday: a service in Seattle in the morning and in Tacoma in the afternoon. This schedule was kept each Sunday without interruption until he graduated in May of 1953.

Ron thoroughly enjoyed his work among the deaf. Many of the deaf brought friends to church and to special rallies. Many accepted invitations to accept Christ as Savior. Many were also baptized in water and in the Holy Spirit. "I never once got 'tongue-tied,'" he said with his fingers crossed.

Offerings were not sufficient to support the ministry's budget. The church headquarters gave DeBock an appointment as a "home missionary" and assisted with financial support of the deaf work. This support came from the Home Missions Department of the Assemblies of God, Springfield, Missouri.

Upon graduation from Northwest Bible College in May of 1953, Ron was offered an interim pastorate at the Assembly of God in Montesano by the Northwest District Council of the Assemblies of God. To accept would mean that he would have to resign the pastorate he held at the two deaf churches.

After considerable prayer over the matter, he contacted Paul and Kathern Carlstrom in Springfield, Missouri. This young couple had a burden for the deaf. They agreed to come to Washington and take over the Seattle and Tacoma deaf congregations which by now had changed their meeting place to Calvary Temple (Seattle) and Evangelistic Tabernacle (Tacoma). The Carlstroms arrived soon thereafter. The DeBocks moved to Montesano in June.

Incidentally, although DeBock was never to serve a church for the deaf after 1953, he found plenty of opportunity to use his sign language proficiency in later assignments in counseling situations, in church and in business.

In retrospect, if Chaplain DeBock had lost his hearing completely in Vietnam, he would have little difficulty communicating. He blames himself for some of his hearing loss. "I failed to put cotton in my ears while working close to the 155s (155 mm cannons) while serving with the 12th Marines (artillery regiment)." Ron is quite upbeat about the matter: "I read lips well," he says.

4

A Chaplain
on Probation?

"For Jehovah God is our Light and our Protector.
He gives us grace and glory.
No good thing will He withhold from those who walk along His paths."
- Psalm 84:11

Some vocations carry with them more risk than others. Shall we say it is easier to get into trouble on some jobs?

Military service is one of those environments! Ask any seasoned veteran of any branch of the armed forces if he ever got into big trouble with the command. He is a rare soldier, sailor or marine who hasn't! Regulations are generally strict, and security tight.

An interesting experience (not at all interesting at the time!) gave Seaman 1st Class Ronald Richardson an introduction to **the Navy way** of disciplinary action.

Army pilot 1st Lieutenant Paul Soules needed flying time in the B-17 in the winter of 1946. (Ron and Paul met while members of the church choir at the Full Gospel Tabernacle in Washington, D. C.)

The plan was to fly to the southwestern United States and return, the roundtrip taking no more than a week. "Care to go along, Ron?" the pilot asked.

"Yes, I sure would. I'll put in for leave," Ron said excitedly.

Leave was granted all right. It would end at midnight Thursday.

But the plane developed a mechanical problem that required attention, delaying passengers and crew an extra day in El Paso. Ron sent a telegram to his command. He had reason to believe this was the proper procedure.

The procedure was correct all right. But whoever received the telegram could not locate it when the plane arrived back in Washington, D. C. on Friday!

Seaman 1st Class Richardson was AWOL! He had sent a wire to the command, but none could be found. When the sailor arrived Friday, they put him in the P.A.L. barracks. (That did not make him a "pal," by the way; Ron was a *Prisoner At Large!*)

Ron did not sing in the choir on Sunday that weekend. Folks at the church had already heard that Ron was in the P.A.L. barracks. Some news travels fast!

Good news came Monday, though. The telegram showed up! Ron looked back on this incident with amusement. But it was not at all amusing at the time!

When someone at church remarked the next Sunday that Ron seemed to be singing better than usual, he replied, "Of course, I've been in **Sing Sing** where the Navy teaches you to sing...I was behind a few bars, but couldn't seem to get the right key!"

That experience was to be helpful years later when Reverend DeBock moved his family to Portland, Oregon, to attend seminary.

It seemed that all of a sudden the young minister was to be humbled like he had never been before, He would be placed on **PROBATION!**

Now the dictionary defines "probation" as a "critical examination and evaluation or subjection of an individual to a period of testing and trial to ascertain fitness (as for a job or school)"

Keep in mind that by this time, Reverend R. G. DeBock had a college degree and had pastored churches for seven years in Washington state. He had already been accepted at Western Evangelical Seminary for graduate study.

But the Registrar of the seminary told him that Advanced Greek could not be taken without first taking Elementary Greek. Ron believed he could handle the advanced course. His transcript also supported this assumption. The Registrar reluctantly acquiesced. "You will be enrolled in the Greek course **ON PROBATION** for the first three weeks," he said.

Soon after enrolling at Western Evangelical Seminary, Ron found a steady job at Portland's main post office. He had applied early and his veteran's points helped to land the position. "You will be **put ON PROBATION** for one year. All employees must wait a year before becoming regulars." He began to think that this "probation" thing is a handy tool and used a lot in the real world!

Soon after DeBock took the post office job to support his family, he received a letter from the Chief of Naval Personnel notifying him of his appointment as a commissioned officer in the Navy Chaplain Corps. In an accompanying letter, the Navy program was explained which would permit the graduate student to go on active duty for training while in seminary, and to go on active duty as a chaplain upon graduation. This program was known as...you guessed it...**"The Ensign Probationary Program."**

Donna and Ron danced around the living room with glee. Even their 6-year-old daughter, Beverly, joined in. The good news? Dad was an ensign in the chaplain corps of the U.S. Naval Reserve.

The bad news? Dad was **ON PROBATION** (again)...in three different areas at the same time! Wow! Will he make it? Stay tuned in!

5

Ministry
Aboard Ships

"And then there are the sailors sailing the seven seas,
plying the trade routes of the world. They, too, observe
the power of God in action. He calls to the storm winds;
the waves rise high. Their ships are tossed to the heavens
and sink again to the depths; the sailors cringe in terror.
They reel and stagger like drunkards and are at their wit's end.
Then they cry to the Lord in their trouble, and He saves them.
He calms the storm and stills the waves. What a blessing is that stillness,
as He brings them safely into harbor! Oh, that these men would praise the Lord
for His loving kindness and for all of His wonderful deeds!
- Psalm 107:23-31

Sea duty for a sailor can be either full of high adventure or sheer drudgery depending upon his perspective.

Navy chaplains are normally assigned to destroyer duty early in their careers. Typically the assignment will be to a division of four ships or to a squadron of eight ships. (This type of naval vessel is nicknamed a "tin can" for the way it bobs up and down in the water.)

Chaplain Ron DeBock received orders to Destroyer Division 232, homeported in Long Beach, California, serving as the staff chaplain for the four ships in the Division: USS MADDOX (DD-731), USS BRUSH (DD-745), USS MOORE (DD-747) and USS PRESTON (DD-795). From the perspective of this energetic 32-year old minister of the Gospel, it was the right place at the right time for him to serve aboard ships. Ron sensed a kind of destiny in what he was doing. He had prepared long and hard for the privilege of ministering to military peronnel and, despite the separation from family, here was an excellent means of fulfilling his calling.

With family settled in a rental house in Long Beach, Chaplain DeBock left on a Western Pacific Cruise with the ships. At sea, he went from one ship to another by helo or high line.

By helo was euphoniously called the "holy helo hop." On a Sunday at sea, arrival by helicopter required a sizeable work party. This translated into the fact that nearly all personnel aboard knew that the chaplain was arriving to conduct worship services!

DeBock was lowered by a sling which fit tightly under the armpits. Soon his feet touched the fantail of the tin can. The return was by the same mode of transportation. Two things must be remembered: (1) Keep your elbows down, and (2) Be sure you clear the life line on lift off.

Ron's para-German word for transfer by helo will help illustrate it: **ein schlingenschwingenhelplessgedanglen mittsuddenishjerkenundarmpitsgetearen!**

Destroyers often escorted a carrier. The carrier usually kept a helicopter on board. Without a helo, the chaplain or others would transfer at sea in the "boatswain's chair." This was a gondola-like chair suspended from a cable. Getting wet happens when one or both ships yaw during the operation.

Ron's para-German word for transfer by bosun's chair vividly tells it: **ein bobbenflippensplashengedunken mittpanikischhopenmeinGottnichtforsaken!**

One Sunday at sea, Chaplain DeBock requested a helo for a morning worship service aboard the BRUSH, but for some reason the signals got mixed and, unknown to the padre, he was lowered onto the MADDOX instead. None of this would have mattered greatly except the sermon he planned to preach on the BRUSH was the same one he got such a good response from the previous week on the MADDOX. So from the moment Ron spotted the MADDOX crew on the fantail until he reached the messdecks where the altar would be rigged, he changed his message. (Incidentally, some said it was the most effective sermon they had heard from the chaplain). Whoever said, "Necessity is the mother of invention?"

But the primary work for a destroyer chaplain is by no means what is done in the worship service. Counseling is the big thing. Counseling and prayers. Sea duty is for some a lonely experience. Mail from home can be disturbing. Much of this counseling is just being a good listener with a knack for knowing where to go for solutions. Chaplain DeBock formed a habit of having prayer at the conclusion of most counseling sessions. He believed that Jesus is the answer to most problems.

An example of the type of problem that can arise aboard ship was experienced by the chaplain, himself. His 9-year old son, Gary, fell off his bicycle and broke a piece off his front tooth. Gary's mother wrote two letters about the mishap. The first letter stated the details of the fall, but the second letter merely suggested that Ron send a thank you to her brother **for taking Gary to the doctor.** Fine. OK. But the first letter did not arrive until two days after the second letter arrived!

One of the ships in the division requested evening prayers be given by the chaplain over the One MC (ship's public address system). This was given into a microphone in the pilot house. DeBock liked the practice and continued with evening prayers aboard that ship whenever he was aboard at sea. Then an interesting thing happened...

The ship was engaged in maneuvers which called for "darken ship." This meant that in the pilot house only a red flashlight could be used and no other. Chaplain DeBock made it a practice to type these prayers on a 3" X 5" card in red ink.

It simply never occurred to Ron that this would pose a problem. But...you guessed it...The boatswain's mate blew his shrill whistle, followed by his familiar announcement: "Now

stand by for evening prayers! " DeBock came up to the microphone with his red flashlight, pulled out his card...and...
NOTHING...ZERO! Again, enough favorable comments about
the prayer made Ron wonder if he should dispense with notes
altogether for preaching and praying.

A chief petty officer had been growing a beard for a long
time. It was a beauty! But along came a directive from the
Fleet Commander (during the "People to People" program)
which forbade naval personnel from going ashore in a foreign
port while wearing a beard. The ships were heading for Kobe,
Japan, where they would remain over Christmas.

Chaplain DeBock arranged for a program complete with
choir which would sing Christmas carols along Kobe's **Sanno-
miya Moto-machi,** a shopping center. All participants were
from ship's company. But he needed a Santa Claus to complete the program. Permission was granted to permit the chief
to go ashore, wearing a Santa Claus outfit. Welfare and Recreation funds were used to get his beard bleached to (wavy)
white.

The chief walked casually ahead of the choir, handing out
candy canes and small, gift-wrapped packages. The choir
stopped at times to sing the carols. DeBock had them sing
"Jingle Bells" in Japanese...and it went over big! "O, Come All
Ye Faithful" was another favorite. From out of nowhere, a
pretty Japanese woman handed a wrapped gift to the chief
(Santa Claus) and said, **"Okurimono, dozo, anata no tame
ni."** (Please take this gift; it is for you.)

DeBock's ship pulled into Sasebo where it was to be
moored at the small Japanese port for at least a week. Since
Ron knew the ship's itinerary would permit a long weekend
retreat, he arranged for several of the men to go with him to a
mountain resort. But they no sooner got settled in when a
message from the ship arrived cancelling all liberty and requiring all personnel to return to the ship immediately for the
purpose of going to sea to ride out an imminent typhoon.

Some might question such logic, of course. Wouldn't it be
best for all concerned to remain in port? No, the American
ship might damage the foreign port's pier. Or the destroyer

itself may get damaged. At any rate, to sea it was. That's the Navy way! More water over the bridge!

As long as we are up to our neck in sea stories, you'll like the exchange between the skipper[7] of the U.S.S. MADDOX and the DesDiv 232[8] chaplain.

During a cruise in Pacific waters, three destroyers in the Division were escorting a flat top.[9] Ron had been riding the U.S.S. BRUSH for more than a week. He came aboard the MADDOX and kept very busy talking with and counseling with men in the afternoon. It got to be chow time[10] and Ron headed for the wardroom.[11]

As the officers sat waiting for the captain, Ron noticed the menu called for fried chicken, his favorite dish. As he sat down, the captain smiled broadly at seeing Ron again.

"Would you like to say a little grace for us, chaplain?" he asked.

(After grace) "What brings you aboard the MADDOX, padre?" the captain enquired.

"I go where I'm needed most, captain." Ron replied. "By the way, you had fried chicken the last time I had a meal here. It's very good!"

"Where have you been, chaplain? We could have used you around here," the XO[12] chimed in.

"I've been riding the BRUSH for about a week," Ron answered.

"So you like our chicken, do you, padre?" the captain butted in.

"Yes, captain," Ron said, "As far as I'm concerned, a bird in the MADDOX is worth two in the BRUSH!" After the laughter, the captain assured Chaplain DeBock that he could ride the MADDOX anytime he wanted.

Some ports of call on the WestPac (Western Pacific) Cruise were Hong Kong, Yokosuka, Subic Bay (Philippine Islands) and Pearl Harbor.

A new commodore came aboard. Each ship has a commanding officer. A commodore has command of the entire division, which in this case was four destroyers. Being a devout Roman Catholic, the new commodore called for the chaplain to meet him in his stateroom.

"You don't have to report everything to me, chaplain," he said. "If you will just stop in to see me once in awhile, we'll have coffee together. Then you can let me know how things are going. After all, I know that you will be out there somewhere working for our Lord!"

Arrival back at Long Beach was a wonderful experience. Absence does make the heart grow fonder! Children have grown taller...and wiser. Our wives have grown lonelier, too!

Sundays in port was much different from sea duty. Worship services were held for all of the ships moored in a nest. Ron was fortunate due to the fact that a close friend, Reverend Fulton Buntain, was in Long Beach, California. He was pastor of the Assembly of God in the city. Young people from his church were encouraged to come aboard for church services. Sunday evenings were very special as the youth brought their musical talents with them. Services were rotated among the ships of the division while in port.

Despite the long separation from family and friends, destroyer duty was very exciting and memorable. The two years went by quickly!

Orders arrived for Ron's next duty station. From sea duty to the Naval Air Station at Memphis was indicative of the wide variety of assignments available to chaplains in the U. S. Navy.

On receiving his Memphis orders, Ron sent a wire to friends back in Puyallup. It simply read: "NEW ORDERS TO MEMPHIS. PSALM 34:6"

6

With Marines In Vietnam

"A thousand shall fall at thy side,
and ten thousand at thy right hand;
but it shall not come nigh thee."
- Psalm 91:7

The Vietnam War was a lengthy, unsuccessful action by South Vietnam and the United States to put a halt to the effort of the Communists of North Vietnam to reunite the nation under one government.

When Viet Minh soldiers (who were well-trained in the North) returned to the South, they instigated guerrilla warfare in the region. They were known as **Viet Cong** and became a growing menace to the Army of the Republic of Vietnam (ARVN).

Although for American fighting troops the Vietnam War did not begin until President Lyndon Johnson responded to the Gulf of Tonkin incident by ordering naval planes to bomb North Vietnam, U.S. military advisers were authorized by President John Kennedy to fight with the ARVN as early as

1961. In August of 1964 the North Vietnamese patrol boats fired on the USS MADDOX (DD-731), the flagship for Destroyer Division 232.

The war escalated rapidly in early 1965 and in March marines landed near Da Nang. At this time Chaplain DeBock was assigned to the 12th Marine Regiment (Artillery) of the 3rd Marine Division based on Okinawa. Chaplain John O'Connor was the Assistant Division Chaplain. After an exemplary career, he would one day become an archbishop in New York.

DeBock landed in Vietnam early in the war. He was one of the chaplains accompanying Marine combat battalions, landing at Da Nang in June of 1965. Navy Chaplains may be assigned to units of the U.S. Marines as well as to the U.S. Coast Guard. "By July 1965 the number of U.S. combat troops had reached 75,000."[13]

DeBock's duties consisted primarily in counseling. Worship services were held when possible. Sunday was not necessarily the best day for scheduling worship. Counseling immediately prior to reconnaissance was particularly important and meaningful in the field. Visits to the small Da Nang hospital were made daily or more frequently as the need dictated. Prayers of a private or group nature were frequently appropriate.

Memorial services were held rarely since the ever-present danger of enemy fire made any open gathering of large numbers of men unwise. During one open field memorial service, one of the men yelled "FIRE!" DeBock abruptly concluded the service with an "Amen," and the marines sped to their battle stations.

The Viet Cong were not the only enemy in the area that slithered on belly. Ron's tent was rigged with a wooden floor. Under his cot was a box where the chaplain kept much of his gear. He returned to his tent one day to find he was challenged by a lowdown fellow — not by a Viet Cong, but a baby cobra! Very colorful. Not large, just a baby.

"You hold the sack, chaplain," the medical service officer said to Ron. "And I'll put him in the sack for study." (It was his job to identify such critters). Ron decided it was the chaplain's job **to stay out of the way!** Incidentally, Chaplain DeBock learned that a baby cobra is as poisonous when young as when full grown!

DeBock opened a box from home with some delicious home-made chocolate chip cookies inside. Even after passing them around, the box was still half full. He tucked the box neatly into the pasteboard box under his cot. Few campers would anticipate what was to follow. Returning to his tent after three or four hours, Ron found a trail of shiny black ants marching away from his cookie box, each carrying a piece of cookie, marching single file to a destination unknown. All they lacked was a drill sergeant and marching band!

Looking back on his first tour in the Da Nang area of Vietnam, Chaplain DeBock felt he was probably most effective while counseling one-on-one, especially with the men who were wounded in the hospital. The climate was hot and muggy. Preparation for such situations was exactly what training was all about, something for which the Marines are famous.

Returning to Vietnam in 1969 after two years' service in Seattle and two more in Japan, DeBock was assigned again to the 3rd Marine Division. This tour his battalion was situated at Dong Ha near the DMZ [14] at the 17th parallel.

A dozen Marines were poised to go on "recon"[15] and met with their chaplain for prayer. DeBock asked them their first names. (First names are seldom convenient in combat situations). Ron knew that more than half of these men had already earned a Purple Heart. Of the twelve, three of the men in the recon group were named "Gary," which inevitably conjured up memories of the chaplain's own 16-year-old **Gary** back home in Puyallup.

A memorial service held at Dong Ha one afternoon had to be cut off abruptly due to rocket fire. Incoming rounds were suddenly evident to some standing there. Ron heard something whistle by which instantly meant two things: (1) They missed again, and (2) It's time to move!

Telltale evidence of incoming rockets was found in the

Dong Ha Chapel. That evening a piece of shrapnel was discovered lodged in the chalice on the altar. If the Catholic Chaplain had been celebrating mass at the time the rocket struck, he might not have survived.

Ron felt good about serving with the Marines at Da Nang in 1965. He even preferred ministering to men in combat situations to many other assignments simply because he felt his ministry was more significant.

During the four years between Ron's first and second tours in Vietnam, his attitude toward the war gradually changed. His views and opinions of the Vietnam War in terms of the worthwhileness of America's involvement changed from **probably worthwhile** in 1965 to **very probably not worthwhile** in 1969. Perhaps his views ran somewhat parallel with the majority opinion among Americans. Who is to say? Ron grappled with the matter.

DeBock knew that "war policies" must be left with the command, where they belonged. A common gripe among Marines was that they were not permitted to fire offensively, for the most part. This was also a matter being debated among politicians back in the states, of course. Ron was a fan of the late General MacArthur, the old soldier with the "wage wars to win" philosophy.

Chaplain DeBock was about to get caught up in another battle as a result of his change of attitude toward America's involvement...and his own. The skirmish opened up some very interesting differences of opinion between DeBock, his church and the Navy.

At least three questions emerged from Ron's change of attitude about the war in Vietnam. First, should Ron have kept quiet about his feelings of less than good conscience concerning America's involvement in the Vietnam conflict? Second, did he receive the proper counsel, support and wisdom from his church concerning his changed position? Third, was Ron's response to his church fitting and proper?

It is hoped that the reader has been furnished with enough written material from the parties to follow the skirmish and to form his own conclusion in answer to the above questions.

This material includes letters from Ron to his church and to the Navy together with responses from each. It includes letters from the Assemblies of God Commission on Chaplains to Ron over a period of eighteen months requesting that he voluntarily resign from active duty in the Naval Reserve without regard to loss of benefits. Ron refused to resign.

During the entire exchange of correspondence, it is noteworthy that cordiality prevailed. Despite bold differences of opinion, all parties maintained a high level of courteous rapport. In the end, Ron did not withdraw from the fellowship of his church or resign his credentials of ordination.

DeBock was not only assigned to perform the duties of a chaplain, but to represent his denomination in the military. He expressed his concerns about the Vietnam war in a candid letter to Rear Admiral James W. Kelly, then serving as the Navy's Chief of Chaplains. In the letter, Ron questioned the relevance of the war itself, about the taking of human lives, and about his less than good conscience about his own involvement. He also requested reassignment, fully aware that such request would not be in his best interest from a career standpoint.

It should be emphasized that all during the year and a half period from the beginning of the exchange of correspondence between Ron, his church, and the Navy, Ron carried out his chaplaincy duties as energetically and intensely as was his style on previous assignments. Fitness reports from his respective commands confirmed this.

Ron was totally convinced that, under the circumstances, God would give him a new signal when needed. This would be in keeping with the promise that the steps of a good man are ordered by the Lord. When months later he received such a clear signal, Ron was surprised at its call for a new direction. **"Practice what you preached."** The call would find DeBock eager to follow his new marching orders!

The war was not going well near the demilitarized zone where Ron was assigned to the 3rd Marine Division in 1969. In his opinion, the casualties seemed exorbitant. Again, the chaplain was not a line officer with any frame of reference to make such a judgment. He was to minister. He knew the difference. Ron wrote a letter to Reverend Bert Webb, then Chairman of the Assemblies of God Commission on Chaplains:[16]

> "Vietnam has done for me what no other kind of experience could possibly do. In years past there was the enchantment of the chaplaincy. The chaplain in combat knows none of this. His energies are drained in the heat of the day in getting to know his men and being *their* chaplain, their pastor and their confessor at times. I began for a time to even wonder if I belonged on the killing team. Was I truly a noncombatant, encouraging the Marines to get on with the job that had to be done? I shared some of my uncertainties with Chaplain Kelly by letter. He has not yet responded to my recent correspondence."

The flak got bad for DeBock. No, it wasn't from the VC[17] or from the Viet Minh guerillas. It began as the result of the conscience letter to Chaplain Kelly.

DeBock felt that he had not one, but two commissions. The first one was to be found in the Gospel of St. Matthew:[18]

> *"And Jesus came and spake unto them, saying, All power is given unto me in heaven and in earth. Go ye therefore, and teach all nations, baptizing them in the name of the Father, and of the Son, and of the Holy Ghost: Teaching them to observe all things whatsoever I have commanded you: and, lo, I am with you alway, even unto the end of the world. Amen."*

The second commission was from The President of the United States of America:[19]

> "To all who shall see these presents greeting: Know Ye, that reposing special trust and confidence in the patriotism, valor, fidelity and abilities of **RONALD G. DeBOCK** I do appoint him a Reserve Officer in the grade of **LIEUTENANT COMMANDER IN THE CHAPLAIN CORPS of the United States Navy** to rank as such from the FIRST day of JANUARY ,

nineteen hundred and SIXTY-SIX. This officer will therefore carefully and diligently discharge the duties of the office to which appointed by doing and performing all manner of things thereunto belonging…"

DeBock never had any doubts concerning why he was in Vietnam serving with combat Marines. He was in Vietnam due to orders from the Chief of Naval Personnel and because it was the will of God. It was not that he particularly **liked** combat zone duty. He neither liked it nor disliked it. His primary motivation was to be in the will of his heavenly Father, Who led him through years of study and experience to this point in time. (Not much different than for many of those with whom he was serving in Vietnam!) Ron believed that destiny had something to do with it all, even the anguish of soul which tested his resolve in the face of suffering and KIAs.[20] He felt so sure of the duty being right for him that he volunteered for a third tour with the same 3rd Marine Division in Vietnam before finishing his second tour "in country."[21]

Soon the Assemblies of God (Ron's church) entered the foray. The flak grew worse. Correspondence flew!

Ron's church wanted him to resign from active duty. This was the same church which would gain fame for defrocking such ministers as Jim Bakker,[22] Richard Dortch,[23] and Jimmy Swaggart.

How many times the Marine Chaplain heard, "War is hell!" To this he would say, "Anyone who has ever said that has experienced only the **war** part. Only **hell** is hell!" This was an important distinction to DeBock in the light of his commission to win souls for his Savior, Jesus Christ.

An amateur chess player, Ron DeBock instinctively knew the rules were not even for both sides of the Vietnam conflict. Marine commanders were fighting under orders which essentially prohibited them from firing until fired upon. This was not at all like the war our American troops waged after the bombing of Pearl Harbor. There was a great deal of uncertainty among the nation's leadership concerning the propriety of our continued involvement. Added to this was the growing drug problem faced by troops in Vietnam and the scenario became even more unpleasant. It was not a matter of questioning the relative power of the (chess) pieces, but the rules of checkmate!

DeBock's initial "conscience letter" to Chaplain Kelly was enough to cause the Assemblies of God Commission on Chaplains to request the chaplain to resign from active duty.

At this point, it must be emphasized that Ron had no quarrel with his church. He never had anything but respect and love for the Assemblies of God. He was as committed to his denominational ordination and calling as an Assemblies of God minister as he was in early years of ministry. Since his ordination in April of 1953, Ron DeBock had never failed to apply for the annual renewal of his "Ordained Fellowship Card." And each year that fellowship card was renewed and Ron carried it proudly and humbly.

From the time Ron wrote to Chaplain Kelly in September of 1969, until his separation from active duty in June of 1971, he never held a grudge or lost faith in the General Council of the Assemblies of God. The sequence of events during this interesting period is revealing. All of the events were carried by correspondence:

Sep 1969   Ron withdraws his request for reassignment in a letter to Chaplain James Kelly, Chief of Navy Chaplains

Sep 1969   In another letter to Chaplain Kelly, Ron affirms his willingness to continue duty in Vietnam or be released from active duty as provided in the BuPers Manual.[24]

Dec 1969   Ron gives Thomas Zimmerman, General Superintendent of the Assemblies of God, permission to review his Service Record in BuPers.[25]

Mar 1970   The Assemblies of God Commission on Chaplains recommends that DeBock accept severance without question "in order to protect severance pay rights."

Apr 1970 Ron explains to the AG Commission that only "regulars" have severance pay rights, and that as a member of the Naval Reserve, he had no severance pay rights.

May 1970 Ron was granted Annual Leave to the Continental United States (from Vietnam).

Jun 1970 Ron tells the AG Commission in Springfield, MO, that he may be able to meet with them in Sep '70.

Jun 1970 The AG Commission state they are not aware of "the new orders which permit you to remain on active duty." (from the late T. E. Gannon, then Chairman of the AG Commission).

Aug 1970 Ron is assigned duty at Great Lakes, Illinois.

Oct 1970 Ron meets with the AG Commission. The Commission informs the Navy Chief of Chaplains that they will ask DeBock to seek for a release from active duty by transferring to the inactive reserve status effective 1 February 1971.

The war in Vietnam was still expanding in the spring of 1970. For Ron, however, it was history. He was grateful for those he touched with counseling and for God's saving grace and merciful protection. For Ron, Vietnam was over. He was in the war at the beginning at Da Nang and near the ending when he packed supplies for his next assignment. Ron left with a prayer for those who would enter combat where he could not be with them...and again, for God's protection. Ron did not lose his life...only a little hearing...and he can live with that. But he might need to change vocations. (Let's not get ahead of the story!)

Of course, the action of the Assemblies of God Commission on Chaplains in requesting that Chaplain DeBock request release from active duty carried with it some incredible blessings which neither Ron nor the AG Commission at that time could possibly know or appreciate.

For one thing, Ron was humbled to think that his peers considered him now unfit to remain on active duty as a navy chaplain. To be sure, he went before his Lord in prayer.

Through it all, Ron felt only a sense of destiny in the making. And through it all, he never felt like "fighting the commission's decision."

But there was clearly disagreement between parties. And some lessons can be learned from disagreements and from differences of opinions. In the work of the Lord, we cannot afford to forget that God is working everything out for our good if we are the called according to His purpose.[26] But, also, we do well to take no vengeance, which our Lord considers His prerogative.[27]

Two letters set forth the disagreement. First, here are pertinent excerpts from a letter from the AG Commission:[28]

"I am deeply disappointed, Brother DeBock, that when our Commission sought to obtain an additional time for you before you would leave the service, and in all sincerity give you our best judgment in the matter, that you would take it in what seems to be a very light and insignificant way and feel that it would be your prerogative to determine anywhere between now and after the holidays as to whether or not you wish to abide by the counsel of your brethren.

"Of course, you would not know this, but I happen to know that when it appeared that you would take the counsel of your brethren and immediately inform the Chief your decision, your name had been submitted to a position which would have provided you an excellent ministry in the event you were leaving the military in the very near future. After your letter was received at headquarters and it became known that as yet you hadn't made a decision, this recommendation for the position that was open has now become void.

"It may be hard for you to understand when I speak as plainly as I do in this letter, that we are anxious to help you and want to do anything we can for you, but, Brother DeBock, I was very sincere when I expressed to the Chief that we still had confidence in your ministry.

"I am not trying to be hard, Brother DeBock, but as far as our Commission is concerned we need to know now and not after the first of the year what your decision is."

For more than a year at this point, the Assemblies of God Commission on Chaplains had been requesting that DeBock request release from active duty. Ron knew the late Brother Gannon to be a gracious gentleman and appreciated the tone of the Chairman's letter.

Chaplain Vincent J. Lonergan, then the Director of the Chaplains Division in the Bureau of Naval Personnel reiterated in a letter to Ron:[29]

"There is no moral pressure to hold you to the (Active Duty) contract. The position of the Chief of Chaplains has always been to honor the request for release from active duty of any Chaplain who so petitions. Your request for release from active duty consonant with the desires of your Church, would be positively received in this office.

"May God bless you during this time of decision and transition."

The lines were drawn. A chaplain had sinned. But it was not unpardonable. Nevertheless, both the chaplain's ecclesiastical endorsing agency and the Chaplains Division of the Department of the Navy were poised to accept DeBock's request for release from active duty.

"What have we got here?" Ron mused. In another day, another Ronald (far and away more articulate) might have said, "Here we go again!"

Somehow it reminded Ron of another chess game. He not only had the knights in shining armor (from BuPers) with swords drawn against him, but the bishops in Springfield were lined up with his King. For sure, DeBock was not about to let anybody use him as a pawn on the board or to "rook" him out of earned military benefits. It appeared they were soon to enter the end game.

Through it all, Ron felt good about the potential outcome. He had learned that his Shepherd not only walked with him on the hillsides, but leads beside the still waters![30] And back at Dong Ha, Ron knew the meaning of another Psalm:[31]

> *"A thousand shall fall at thy side, and ten thousand at thy right hand; but it shall not come nigh thee."*

Beyond that, Chaplain DeBock was thoroughly convinced that "he which hath begun a good work in you will perform it until the day of Jesus Christ."[32]

Ron's response to Chairman Gannon's letter was to the effect that he would have completed almost seventeen years of federal service should he complete his current contract with the Navy. He also cited his Active Duty Agreement obligating him to serve for the full period of active duty specified, which was 31 August 1972. Then, he quoted from the BuPers Manual:[33]

> "Requests for early release will not be approved un-less an officer has completed one year of duty at his current duty station." (Chaplain DeBock reported for duty at Great Lakes September, 1970).

DeBock's response continued:[34]

Above all, I want to observe the spirit of the law!
"The Commission has requested, in effect, that I vol-untarily resign from active duty without regard to loss of earned benefits. Aside from the fact that I love the chaplaincy and the Navy which has made my life's ministry possible, there are other reasons…why I cannot seek release at this time. First, I believe it would be legally and morally wrong to disregard obligated service under my contract. The Navy ex-pects me to live up to my obligations. Most pastors

and within our denomination I presume nearly all General Council officers and other employees serve under some kind of contract. It doesn't seem fair to deprive me of the same contractual rights. Also, I am assigned to a chapel here which offers a great challenge and a wonderful opportunity for service to my Lord. God's blessing on our chapel activities is obvious at a glance of attendance graphs and the expanded circle of outreach by workers.

"As an ordained minister of the Assemblies of God I am blessed with the privileges and courtesies which accompany that high calling. Likewise, as a lieutenant commander in the U.S. Naval Reserve, I enjoy certain rights and benefits with other officers. They are substantial and I am aware of them.

"Finally, Brother Gannon, the Commission's expression of 'confidence in your ministry' is appreciated. I feel quite sure that the Chief of Chaplains understands that the counsel of the brethren was no reprimand as you were careful to explain in your letter to him...

"Since our Commission has thoughtfully assured the Chief of Chaplains in this manner, I shall endeavor to minister in a spirit and manner which will bring only credit to our church, by the grace of God."

The Assemblies of God Commission on Chaplains was disappointed that Ron did not resign from active duty. Chairman Gannon wrote,[35]

"I must confess to you that I am deeply disappointed that you do not find room in your heart to accept the counsel and wisdom of your brethren regarding this matter.

"I know of no pastor, district council officer or General Council officer who has any contract. In fact, any office can be declared vacant under proper circumstances. When such action is taken, there is no mustering out pay, no moving expenses, and as a rule, not more than 30 days to make the change."

Ron did not attempt to verify the facts of the last paragraph of Chairman Gannon's letter. The comparison did not seem to fit his case. The worst case scenario did not seem to jibe with the Navy's treatment of its active personnel. It was also contrary to Ron's experience with civilian churches. Therefore, he looked upon the letter with a measure of disbelief. He expected the Navy to consider his years of service in its determination of separation pay and moving expenses. Besides, Ron had no intention of resigning from active duty.

Hindsight revealed that the Navy would grant generous separation benefits to Ron which far exceeded the observations described by his church. The Navy allowed both moving expenses and two month's basic pay for each year of active duty. The latter was non-taxable due to a service-connected disability, the hearing loss suffered in Vietnam.

Superintendent Richard Dortch (of PTL fame) invited Ron to speak at the Illinois District Council. He also received a warm congratulatory letter from General Superintendent Thomas Zimmerman dated a day later. Ron appreciated the spirit of goodwill extended by the Assemblies of God. Both of these letters appear in the appendix. The sequence of events continued:

15 Dec 1970   R. J. Carlson, Northwest District Superintendent, requests meeting with the AG Commission on Ron's behalf.

21 Dec 1970   AG Commission advises RADM Garrett, Chief of Chaplains, of special session 5 Jan 1971

24 Dec 1970   Chaplain Frank Darkowski, Director, Chaplains' Dept., Great Lakes, tells Chief of Chaplains that "Chaplain DeBock has fulfilled his assignments in an excellent to outstanding manner."

5 Jan 1971   AG Commission meets in special session. R. J. Carlson was present. Due to a snowstorm, Ron was unable to get plane reser-

	vations. A four-point decision was submitted by the Commission.
26 Jan 1971	R. J. Carlson informs DeBock that he gained a point of appeal left open before endorsement would be withdrawn.
Jan 1971	Ron enters Naval Hospital, Great Lakes, for hearing tests.
Feb 1971	Ron is transferred to Naval Hospital, Philadelphia for continued audio testing. After 61 days of hospitalization and testing, Ron was offered a medical separation.
Mar 1971	Chaplain DeBock returns to duties at Forrestal Village Chapel, Naval Training Center, Great Lakes, Illinois. Pre-Easter chapel activities keep him busy.
1 Jun 1971	Ron receives BuPers Order NR 137878 entitled **"Separation from Active Duty"**
10 Jun 1971	Ron is detached from active duty.

Vietnam veterans are more prone to suicide and premature death from auto accidents, compared with men who did not serve in the military, according to a study by physicians at the University of California Medical Center, San Francisco. The article was carried by the Los Angeles Times. Compared with non-veterans, Vietnam veterans may be 86 percent more likely to die from suicide and 53 percent more likely to die from motor vehicle accidents. The report documents in Vietnam veterans, according to the article, the magnitude of the so-called post-traumatic stress disorder, which includes a variety of psychological and health-related problems that have been linked to wartime military service.

Meanwhile, an interesting article appeared on the Opinion page of The Morning News Tribune which was written by Fred Grimm, a columnist with the Miami Herald. The article was written at the height of the 1992 political campaign and suggests that the Vietnam War made liars out of lots of us.[36]

"It was 1969. The nation was divided, protesters were marching...

"We had become a country in which young men feigned insanity to avoid induction. They became cross-dressers. Went to Canada. Claimed narcotic addictions. They faked ailments, handicaps and sexual perversions, desperate to be declared unfit for military service.

"Clutching student deferments, near idiots crowded into colleges, where deans became God-like arbitrators, deciding who would be attending the winter semester and who would be tiptoeing among the punji sticks.

"The Vietnam War spawned a national weirdness, a sort of allpervasive antiwar pop culture.

"But by 1992, the madness that Vietnam inflicted on the country has been reduced to an innocuous shorthand: 'unpopular war.'

"Sunday morning TV's celebrity journalists talk of how Bill Clinton and Dan Quayle dealt with Vietnam and offhandedly mention that it was 'an unpopular war.' As if that could explain why men cut off parts of fingers before draft physicals…

"Bill Clinton faced a simple question: Do you want to go to Oxford on a Rhodes Scholarship? Or would you rather go to Vietnam?

"Quayle says he got no special help getting his National Guard slot and didn't join to avoid Vietnam."

Vietnam in Retrospect

Ron DeBock came on active duty as a navy chaplain in June 1960, long before America sent in fighting troops. Like all chaplains, he *volunteered* to serve his country. Like other chaplains, he was at the same time serving his Lord as well. A double commission, so to speak.

DeBock was already assigned to the 12th Marines, an artillery regiment on Okinawa, when the Vietnam conflict flared up. New orders were, therefore, unnecessary to put him in Country in April of 1965. The chaplain just went into the Da Nang area with the marine regiment.

Believe it or not, Ron DeBock does not feel any more patriotic for having served his country in Vietnam. He was merely fulfilling his God-given assignment. Nor does he consider the explanations given by either Governor Bill Clinton or Vice President Dan Quayle should be construed as less patriotic. And Ron would agree that it was an unpopular war. It was unpopular in the sixties and seventies, too. In the nineties, more so!

"What struck you most in Vietnam, then, Ron?"

"It isn't what struck me that impressed me," he would reply; "it *was what missed me* that I'm thankful for! When 58,183 men and women died in Vietnam, why was I spared?"

No loss of life, joy, peace or sense of destiny
No suicidal tendencies
No post-traumatic stress disorder
No injuries…only loss of hearing and I can live with that.

As for the position which the Assemblies of God Commission on Chaplains took in requesting Ron to pursue inactive reserve status:

(1) Ron appreciated the AG Commission's wisdom and decisions!
    a. It was a complicated call and without precedent.
    b. Ron would never voluntarily resign in the middle of a contract.

(2) Ron appreciated the efforts of the late Reverend R. J. Carlson, Northwest District Superintendent, at a crucial time during the process.

(3) Ron recognized the fact that the AG Commission's action would have some bearing on his denomination's relationship with the Chaplains' Division and future AG chaplains.

(4) Ron was fully prepared psychologically for release from active duty in early 1971.
    a. His "Practice what you preached" commission from the Lord was very much on his mind.
    b. The call he received to serve as Director of Public Relations at Northwest College of the Assemblies

of God in Kirkland, Washington, upon returning home to Puyallup, was a perfect transition to the new call. Dr. D.V. Hurst offered Ron the position less than a week after Ron returned home from Great Lakes.

To young men and women who are called upon to go into combat for their country, Chaplain DeBock would say:

(1) Trust in God with all your heart. Believe that He has your best interest in mind.

(2) Accept Christ as your personal Savior and have courage to meet the enemy as directed by your tactical commander(s).

(3) Remember that Jesus has promised to be with you…no matter where you are called upon to go or to serve!

(4) Take your Bible in your back pack. Read it when you can! Favor the four New Testament Gospels, the Book of Proverbs and the Psalms.

(5) Find out when chapel services are held and worship regularly. (There's more power in praising God than most of us can know!)

MAG-39 Chapel, Quang Tri Vietnam

7

Emphasis On
Praising God

"Oh that men would praise the Lord
for His goodness and for his wonderful works
to the children of men!"
- Psalm 107:15, KJV

For me to omit a chapter on *praise* in my autobiography would be like making a chocolate milkshake without adding the chocolate syrup. I think this lifelong emphasis began with my remembrance of John Dotson who led me to accept Jesus Christ in the Olympia Foursquare Church in November of 1944.

It was Brother Dotson's habit to stand to his feet during testimony times and declare the goodness of God in his life. I noticed that he would often begin or end his testimony by quoting that verse which appears four times in Psalm 107:

"Oh that men would praise the Lord for His goodness, and for his wonderful works to the children of men!"

So, my dear Brother Dotson, to you who became the

57

bearer of the good news of the Gospel that brought redemption and an abundant life in Christ: this chapter is dedicated to you.

The function of praise has taken so many forms that its place in theology today is unclear. In some churches it seems to have been almost unwanted. On the other hand, some of the more exaggerated forms of praise have been associated with emotionalism. The Christian believer who seeks a proper balance in this regard, whether in his private worship or in the worship services of his local church, needs to understand the scope of Christian praise as it is taught in the Scriptures. I don't suppose it is necessary to explain at this point that I hold to the belief that Scriptures in the sixty-six books of the Old and New Testaments comprise the infallible Word of truth for faith and practice.

My interest in the matter of praising God grows out of at least two convictions: First, that nothing is so important to the life of the Christian believer as the assurance that he or she is in the will of God and has the approval of God. Secondly, that God strongly desires that His people recognize their Creator and give Him the glory due to His name. A particular fondness for Biblical poetry, especially for the book of The Psalms has made the subject of praise an interesting one. The Psalms were a continual source of joy and strength since high school days.

Efforts of Communication Between Man and God

When men desire to worship God, to praise Him, or to engage in prayer, a kind of communication is necessary. There can be no satisfactory completion of acts of supplication or of offerings of adoration unless the gap is bridged between the human and the divine.

Many early altars were erected for purposes of worship. The main idea regarding the sacred stone was that it either was actually the abode of deity or indicated the nearby presence of deity.[37] When Jacob awoke from his sleep in which he saw a vision of the ladder with angels ascending and descending, he took the stone which had been his pillow and set it for a pillar, vowing that "If God will be with me…then shall the Lord be my God."[38] The position of the Altar of incense in the sanctuary of the tabernacle lay between the gold candlestick and the table: "It stood immediately if front of the veil, which speaks of the believer-priest's testimony (worship of) to God."[39] (The phrase "believer-priest" is an idea that holds that all believers have a direct approach to God by virtue of their relation to Christ.)[40]

During the third and fourth centuries after Christ, it became popular for men to become hermits or to live in cloisters of only the most pious. Monasticism was a system of renunciation of life in the world for the purpose or promoting the interests of the soul.[41] The disturbing evils of the world interfered with holy worship and escape was, therefore, considered desirable. St. Anthony was the first of these hermits to gain world-wide fame. He lived in seclusion in the desert from age 20 to 106 years and became so popular that hermit life became a mass-movement.[42] Monastic life avoided many temporal concerns in another attempt to keep the lines of communication open between men and God.

The biblical record assures mankind that God has made great efforts to reunite all who have lost fellowship with Him. The Old Testament presents God as walking with His people. He encamped among them. He spoke to them through His prophets. He provided them with the Law as early as Moses' time. Likewise, in the New Testament, Paul's message to the Corinthians emphasized "that God was in Christ reconciling the world unto himself."[43] Thus, God spared not his own Son in making possible salvation for all who believe in Jesus Christ.[44] That salvation is prior to any satisfying relationship with God is Scriptural teaching.

Whether one desired to communicate in the form of prayer, in the form of praise, or to contact the Lord in any manner, he was to do so in the name of Jesus.[45] We can only conclude that our Lord has indeed provided a way into His presence! Men who would make contact with God today are confronted with some of the same problems that had to be faced by believers down through the history of the Christian

Church. This was always a two-way proposition. For man to desire an audience before God, he had to be a "listener" at some time himself. Furthermore, not all have listened when God spoke. Even granting the dedicated efforts of Christ's best ambassadors, there have always been those who refused to hear the truth of the Gospel despite the clarity of its presentation. To receive truth one must truly want it! John explained:

And this is the judgment, that light is come into world, and man loved the darkness rather than the light; for their works were evil. For every one that doeth evil hateth the light, and cometh not to the light, lest his works should be reproved. But he that doeth the truth cometh to the light, that his works may be manifest, that they have been wrought in God.[46]

Such refusal of light as depicted in this passage precludes the possibility of enlightened communication with God. Another hindrance to man's communion with God is his own human limitations. Man, himself, has been ordained to deliver divine truth, the result of which should be the worship of God. Since the time of Christ, each generation called for preachers:

How then shall they call on him in whom they have not believed? and how shall they believe in him whom they have not heard? and how shall they hear without a preacher?[47]

The vocabulary of the preacher becomes a liability rather than an asset in cases where his audience does not comprehend. The problem of mental communication on the human level — that is, man-to-man, is a broad universal problem of which the minister should be aware. It was exposed by Stuart Chase:

Failure of mental communication is painfully in evidence nearly everywhere we choose to look. Pick up any magazine or newspaper and you will find many of the articles devoted to sound and fury from politicians, editors, leaders of industry, and diplomats. You will find the text of the advertising sections devoted almost solidly to a skillful attempt to make words mean something different to the reader from what the facts warrant.[48]

Some of the difficulty here is in the realm of semantics. Words have not meant the same thing to all who heard them. This fact is especially noticeable in the communicating of moral, religious and spiritual ideas.

Closely related to the foregoing is the barrier of language itself. Written originally Hebrew and Greek, the Bible has appeared in numerous translations. Although many are not seriously hindered by the multiplicity of translations, some laymen are, and require the instruction of a patient teacher. The Bible has always been to me the infallible word of God, but it "has worn all sorts of different dresses in different ages and countries."[49]

There are other more practical considerations which affect the atmosphere of communion with God. Whether these are aids or hindrances to the divine/human encounter would, perhaps, be debatable. In the United States, freedom to praise and worship God today is a matter awaiting individual application. Citizens are privileged to worship God in the manner of their own choice. This nation has generally protected this heritage constitutionally and traditionally.

The founding fathers recognized an all-important concern of the historic Augsburg Confession that "It is not necessary that human traditions, rites, or ceremonies instituted by men should be alike everywhere."[50] (Before the states of Arizona, Idaho, Nevada, New Mexico, North Dakota, South Dakota, Utah, Washington, and Wyoming were admitted into the union, they were required to enter a compact with the federal government securing perfect toleration of religious sentiment, and providing that no inhabitant be molested in person or property on account of his or her mode of religious worship.)[51]

Whatever contributes to meaningful worship contributes to man's possibility of making contact with God in a satisfying way. Today's comfortable churches, well-lighted, well-ventilated, with good heating systems have at least reduced some of the physical obstructions to worship. Most churches have taken the acoustical factors into consideration in their architecture and some are equipped with a row of pews where the hard-of-hearing may "tune in" the preacher by simply plugging into an audiophone.

When I visited the Yoido Full Gospel Church in Seoul in October of 1986 and a year later also, I heard Pastor Paul Yonggi Cho's sermon in English from a headphone in the foreigner's section of the balcony. And, although the main sanctuary which seats 25,000 was full, another 25,000 members were worshipping in fifteen small chapels connected by close-circuit television. This thriving church, the largest in the world, joined the U.S.A. Assemblies of God (my own denomination) December 15, 1984.

God's love for man was in Christ, through Whom God provided a ready access to himself. The fellowship broken through the fall of man was restored for all believers in the person of God's Son. The incarnation thus marked God's supreme effort to bridge the widening gap of separation between Himself and man and made communion obtainable in Christ.

The biggest hindrance to man's making any satisfying contact with God in praise and worship seems to be the lack of any real desire to do so.

Early Church Worship

Was there a significant place for the expression of Christian praise in the first and second century worship?

Jesus did not inaugurate any new patterns of worship for the church except for the ordinance of the Lord's Supper. He told the Samaritan woman that "God is a Spirit: and they that worship him must worship in spirit and truth.[52] The elements of instruction, preaching, prayer and breaking of bread were mentioned, and mentioned in such a way as clearly to show that these elements were, from the beginning, the foundation of all the worship life of the Christian community. Arthur Hoyt listed the seven New Testament elements of worship as:

(1) The reading of the Scriptures.
(2) The exposition of the Scripture; teaching or preaching.

(3) Prayer, holding a prominent place, both a use of sacred and venerable forms, and free and spontaneous in expression.

(4) Singing; the peculiar expression of the devotional sentiment, the use of both old and new hymns.

(5) The Creed; the public confession of the faith of Christians and the testimony to the essential facts and truths of the new religion.

(6) The offering; a practical expression of gratitude to God for His great gift, and to men of the new love that was to control human relations.

(7) The Sacraments - two: Baptism and the Lord's Supper; baptism, the outer sign of the inward change of life and the formal intrance into the new Society; the Lord's Supper, with the Agape, used at first with every service of public worship, and with no fixed ritual.[54]

Oscar Cullman noted still other elements from the Pauline Epistles in the very earliest period of worship. These were the Psalms, revelation, speaking with tongues and the interpretation of tongues[55] as mentioned by Paul.[56]

Five examples of praise were found in the New Testament. Three of these were in The Acts while two were in the Gospel of Luke. The Greek word *ainountes*[57] (praising) was used here in the sense of "laudation."[58]

The lame beggar by the temple (Acts 3:8) was praising *(ainwn)* God for the miraculous healing of his lame condition. As soon as his feet and ankle-bones received strength at the hand of Peter and John, he began to give the credit to the Lord:

And leaping up, he stood, and began to walk; and he entered with them into the temple, walking, and leaping, and praising God. And all the people saw him walking and praising God.[59]

The healed beggar accompanied the disciples to the temple where they worshipped God together.

Paul and Silas praised God in prison at Philippi. (Acts 16:25). Several unusual features accompanied the praises of

the missionaries:
   (1) The setting was an extraordinary one and certainly dissimilar to the synagogue or temple environment of worship.
   (2) The hour of midnight was rather late to be engaging in prayer or to be singing praises.
   (3) Paul and Silas were severely beaten not long before they sang praises to God.
   (4) Their feet were in the stocks.
   (5) Prisoners were listening to the missionaries.
   (6) Paul and Silas were under guard, but the jailer went to sleep.

Then there were witnesses to the healing of the blind man at Jericho. (Luke 18:43). Those who saw this great miracle performed by Jesus gave praise to God. The man, too, with his sight, followed Jesus and glorified God. The word **ainon** (praise) is from the same Greek stem **ainos** used in Acts 2:47 and Acts 3:8 meaning "laudation."

Finally, the multitude at the triumphal entry praised the Son of man as He rode humbly into Jerusalem on a colt. (Luke 19:37). They began to rejoice in the streets and to praise God with a loud voice for all the mighty works which they had seen. The form of their praise was: "Blessed is the King that cometh in the name of the Lord: peace in heaven, and glory in the highest."[60] Some of the Pharisees wanted Jesus to rebuke the disciples for such loud outbursts, but the Son of God answered them with "I tell you that, if these shall hold their peace, the stones will cry out."[61] The same Greek form for praise *(ainein)* as seen before was used here in the infinitive form "to laud."

Praising God the Bible Way

Despite the preëminent place given to praising the Lord in the worship of the early Christian church, opinions differ widely when it comes to ascertaining the content of Christian praise. What are its elements? To what extent is man obliged to render praise to God? What expressions of this praise may be considered biblical and, therefore, proper? With these questions in mind, this chapter had its mission to find answers. The answers were essential to preaching and the answers are essential for practicing.

Biblical reference fall generally into two categories: (1) Exhortations to praise and (2) Examples of praise. One must study both of these areas to learn the biblical concept of praise. Beforehand, definitions of what we mean by *"praise"* would be an appropriate place to begin.

Definitions of Praise

A standard dictionary defined praise as an act of man designed "1. To express a favorable judgment of: COMMEND 2: to glorify (a god or saint) esp. by the attribution of perfections."[62]

The International Standard Bible Encyclopaedia added: *Praise may be bestowed upon unworthy objects or from improper motives, but true praise consists in a sincere acknowledgment of a real conviction of worth.*[63]

Praise has been defined by theological writers in various ways. Due to the very nature of the subject, uniformity was not expected and was not found in their definitions! This does not mean that their respective views were in disagreement; but each writer emphasized a different aspect of praise:

C. S. Lewis	"Except where intolerable adverse circumstances interfere, praise almost seems to be inner health made audible."[64]
G. S. Bowes	"What is praise? The rent we owe to God; and the larger the farm the greater the rent should be."[65]
H. Orton Wiley	"Praise is the audible expression which extols the Divine Perfections..."[66]
C. H. Spurgeon	"Praise is the dress of saints in heaven; it is meet that they should fit it on below."[67]
Augustine	"Whatever thou dost, do well, and thou hast praised God."[68]

John Trapp   "...Right principles and upright prac-
                    tices; this is real and substantial prais-
                    ing of God. Thanksdoing is the proof
                    of thanksgiving."[69]

Thus, like a well-cut diamond, each facet of praise contributes to its brilliance. The above definitions indicate vari-
ously an overflow from a full Christian life, a debt, or a way of
life involving personal ethics and moral uprightness. What
tremendous clues for living well!

God Praises Man

At the baptism of Jesus in the Jordan River, a voice was
heard "out of the heavens, Thou art my beloved Son, in thee I
am well pleased."[70] Of course, Jesus welcomed the assurance
that He moved among men under the approval of the Father.

Jesus did not withhold praise when it was called for. He
commended the poor widow for her offering of two mites by
telling the onlookers, "She hath cast in more than they all."[71]
He praised the centurion for his "great faith."[72] Jesus also said
of John the Baptist that there was not a greater prophet than
he among those that are born.[73]

The faithful servant, in the parable which Jesus told of the
pounds, was commended and made ruler over ten cities.
These words of approbation inspired the song "He'll Understand and Say 'Well Done.'"[74] Christians frequently testify
that the hearing of these words from the lips of their Lord will
be the greatest reward they could imagine receiving in heaven:
"Well done, thou good and faithful servant!"[75]

Both God and man engaged in the praise of men, but
there was one basic difference: God's commendations were
always genuine. The praise which men gave, on the other
hand, occasionally degenerated into mere flattery, an example
of improper motivation. Mere flattery was especially disap-
proved in the Proverbs.[76]

God as the Object of Praise

In the Bible it is God who is especially presented as the

object of praise. Every thing that hath breath is to give Him praise.[77] Even the inanimate objects can praise the Lord — rationally only through man's appreciation, however. Biblical references to inanimate objects that give praises to God are the writings of imaginative poets and ought to be understood and appreciated in the light of the Hebrew poetry it is. Another interpretation could lead one to a form of the erroneous doctrine of pantheism.

The Psalmist, David, said clearly "I will call on the Lord, who is worthy to be praised."[78] John refers to Christ in a similar way: "Worthy is the Lamb that was slain to receive power, and riches, and wisdom, and strength, and honour, and glory, and blessing."[79] The very theme of the Psalms is one of praise to God. Again and again comes the exclamation: "Oh that men would praise the Lord for his goodness..."[80] Although it was properly a spontaneous reaction of man to the manifold goodness of God, David found it necessary one day to instruct his soul to call to remembrance God's blessings upon his life.[81]

Do the Scriptures make praising the Lord obligatory? Angels and human beings were assigned to praise the Lord:

Angels	"Bless the Lord, ye his angels, that excel in strength..."[82] "Praise ye him, all his angels..."[83]
Human beings	"Sing unto the Lord, O ye saints of his, and give thanks at the remembrance of his holiness."[84]

John Pulsford went so far as to say:

There is no heaven, either in this world or the world to come for people who do not praise God. If you do not enter into the spirit and worship of heaven, how should the spirit and joy of heaven enter into you?[85]

All humanity was enjoined to praise the Lord: the Gentiles,[86] young men, and maidens; old men, and children;[87] kings of the earth, princes, and judges,[88] masters and servants, small and great.[89] "Let all flesh bless his holy name for ever and ever.[90]

Hebrew poetry reached a zenith in imagination and majesty where nature was mentioned as rendering praise to God. Rather than literalizing the praises that proceed from inanimate things, the reader should recognize the poetic style and take care not to put such praise on a par with the praise from rational beings:

> *Praise ye him, sun and moon: praise him, all ye stars of light. Praise*
> *the Lord from the earth, ye dragons, and all deeps: Fire, and hail:*
> *snow, and vapours; stormy wind fulfilling his word: Mountains, and*
> *all hills; fruitful trees, and all cedars: Beasts, and all cattle; creeping*
> *things, and flying fowl...*[91]

> *Make a joyful noise unto the Lord, all the earth: make a loud noise, and*
> *rejoice, and sing praise. Let the sea roar, and the fulness thereof; the*
> *world, and they that dwell therein. Let the floods clap their hands: let*
> *the hills be joyful together.*[92]

In the light of such spontaneous response of all creation to its Maker, Spurgeon attentively asked:

> *What if men are silent, yet the woods, and seas, and mountains, with*
> *all their countless tribes, and all the unseen spirits that walk them, are*
> *full of the divine praise. As in a shell we listen to the murmurs of the*
> *sea, so in the convolutions of creation we hear the praises of God.*[93]

The prophet Isaiah also described a time in prophetic fulfillment when "...the mountains and the hills shall break forth before you into singing, and all the trees of the field shall clap their hands."[94]

But the praises of nature could scarcely suffice for the praises of men to God. The Bible furnishes many sound reasons to show why men ought to render praise to God. Let us not forget that nature was created and is sustained by the Creator. Though miraculous and wonderful to behold, this creation, all fashioned for the benefit of men and women, has no cause to be thankful for such manifestations of God as his mercy, his salvation, his counsel, or his answering of prayer. Therefore, unless men and women praise the Lord, the Lord remains un-thanked!

Praise is the Duty of Christians

The Bible enjoins all men to praise the Lord, but it is the distinct privilege and responsibility to do so. However, to view Christian praise as an obligation is to overlook one of its basic characteristics. Praise is a part of worship which should flow spontaneously and easily out of a grateful heart. Only a myopic view can visualize either a kind of worship whose chief aim was to fulfill an obligation, or Christian praise given under duress.

Many biblical references point to the responsibility of Christians to render praise to God. Two of my favorites are in Psalm 100 and in the New Testament book of I Thessalonians:

Psalm 100 This well-known Psalm of Thanksgiving furnishes twentyone suggestions for praise-giving hearts: It gives a three-fold reason why all men should be praising the Lord:

(1) **The goodness of the Lord.** God is far better than we could deserve. He was good. He is good. He will be good.

(2) **The mercy of the Lord.** God is unchangeable and everlasting. His forgiveness is ever the same. His grace is faithful.

(3) **The truthfulness of the Lord.** God is true. He is faithful. He can be fully trusted and will never go back on his word.

It is axiomatic that any worthwhile offering of praise to God can only be done by contemplating the greatness of the God to Whom such praise is given! And make no mistake about it: God rewards those who praise him. He did not fail Israel in the hour of their greatest need[95] and the Christian may praise Him for equal faithfulness today and always![96]

I Thessalonians 5:16-18 Paul admonished the saints at Thessalonica to *"Rejoice* evermore; *pray* without ceasing; in everything *give thanks*: for this is the will of God in Christ Jesus to you-ward." No particular mention was made of "praise" here by Paul. Nevertheless, some characteristics which have been noted as belonging to the nature of praise and which are normally associated with biblical praise appear here in terse form. Clearly praise would be incomplete without any one of the three essentials combined in this passage. Biblical cross-references will corroborate this fact:

   (a) David brought the ark of God to Jerusalem with shouts of praise and singing.[97]

   (b) Moses led the Children of Israel in a song of praise after crossing the Red Sea and Miriam led the women in an answering chorus with her timbrel.[98]

   (c) Solomon led Israel in praises to God at the dedication of the temple.[99]

   (d) Paul and Silas prayed and sang hymns unto God in the prison at Philippi.[100]

Rejoicing, prayer, and the giving of thanks appear to be facets of the many-sidedness of praise in the biblical concept.

The passage I Thessalonians 5:16-18 contains a thread of continuity! This affords a stabilizing element, essential for living a consistent life in Christ. What truth can one glean from this "continuation" theme found in such terms as *always, without ceasing,* and *in every thing?* How does it contribute to our experience of praising the Lord? Circumstances certainly have a tendency to discourage one's praises, do they not? Adversity hits. Loved ones are taken. A calamity must be faced. Just as there is a tendency to rejoice only when things go well and to pray only when it seems necessary, so men and women neglect the place of praise when problems come on the scene. The "giving of thanks" in this passage very nearly equals the rendering of praise to God. Paul added that thanks should be given "in every thing" and emphasized that this was the will of God! —

According to Edward Payson, Christians have not been liquidating their debt of praise to God:

> *During every day and every hour which has elapsed since the apostasy of man, this debt (of praise to God) has been increasing; for every day and every hour all men ought to have given unto Jehovah the glory which is due to His name. But no man has ever done this fully. And a vast proportion of our race have never done it at all.*[101]

Similarly, Abraham Wright marks the rendering of praise to God as one of the most neglected duties of believers:

There is hardly any duty more pressed in the Old Testament upon us, though less practiced, than this of praising God.[102]

Praise from Unregenerate Persons

"Praise is comely for the upright,"[103] but what may be said of the unregenerate? Pharisees accused the disciples of Jesus of transgressing the tradition of the elders by eating with unwashed hands. The Son of God replied that they were hypocritically making void the commandments of God for the sake of their traditions. He then likened them to the people foretold in Isaiah's prophecy:

This people honoreth me with their lips; but their heart is far from me.
But in vain do they worship me, teaching as their doctrines the
precepts of men.[104]

The natural man (men and women who have not been born again) does not possess that personal relationship with God which evokes the normal response of praise to his Creator; and praise would not be worthy of the name were it merely lip-service. The unregenerate person would find it difficult to offer acceptable praise to the Lord since there would be lacking a "singleness of heart" for such response.[105] It might be said in either case the responsibility of the un regenerate person to render praise to his Maker is greater than his **response-ability.** For, while God deserves the gratitude of all men, He will receive little from those yet unyielded to the terms and conditions of the Gospel of Jesus Christ.

Delighting in the Praising of God

The Scriptures contain such phrases as "glory in thy praise,"[106] and to "triumph in thy praise."[107] With the recognition of his responsibility and the carrying out of the same by sincere acts of praise to God, the believer soon will have discovered precious return benefits. Praise brings to the believer the deepest satisfactions life offers. I cannot imagine either the "life more abundantly"[108] mentioned by Jesus or the "joy unspeakable and full of glory"[109] experienced by Peter without engaging in such adoration and worship of the Lord.

Not only is it true "as a man thinketh in his heart so is he,"[110] but it is also true "as a man singeth in his heart so is he." (Singing as an expression of praise weaves as a thread throughout the Bible!) To the church at Colosse Paul exhorted:

> *Let the word of Christ dwell in you richly, ... teaching and admonishing one another in psalms and hymns and spiritual songs, singing with grace in your hearts to the Lord.*[111]

This activity is spiritual in nature and is substantially that of delighting in the praise of God, a practice which affords "the desires of thy heart."[112]

Perhaps we should ask what is the deep satisfaction that is derived from praising the Lord. Is it not the inner presence of the Holy Spirit? Those early Christians who daily praised the Lord were often spoken of as being "full of joy and the Holy Ghost."[113] All indicators seem to point to the fact that properly motivated praise to God brings an inner sense of spiritual health. This sense of well-being may be called peace of mind.

Proper Expressions of Praise

Praise is expressed biblically in a variety of ways. What are some of the ways in which men have applauded deity? It is well to bear in mind that modes of expressing praise cannot be considered purely physical or mechanical. The mouth and lips merely speak audibly one's feelings in the heart. The Psalmist found it difficult to express his adoration for God: "Who can utter the mighty acts of Jehovah, or show forth all his praise?"[114] Words alone seemed insufficient for Paul, too, for he wrote: "Thanks be to God for his unspeakable gift."[115]

Worshipers frequently sang a hymn, prayed or testified. These modes of expressing praise seemed to fall into two categories: **(1) Vocal Praise,** including song, testimony, prayer, shouting, and **(2) Instrumental Praise.** A combination of the two also appear in the Scriptures.

72

Vocal Praise

The Psalmist observed:

Because thy lovingkindness is better than life, my lips shall praise thee. My lips shall utter praise, when thou hast taught me thy statutes.[116]

O Lord, open thou my lips; and my mouth shall shew forth thy praise. My soul shall be satisfied as with marrow and fatness; and my mouth shall praise thee with joyful lips.[117]

(1) Worshipping the Lord With Singing

The Apostle Paul urged the believers at Ephesus to

...be filled with the Spirit; speaking to yourselves in psalms and hymns and spiritual songs, singing and making melodies in your heart to the Lord; giving thanks always for all things unto God and the Father in the name of our Lord Jesus Christ.[118] *People of God, because ye are saints: and if sinners are wickedly silent, let your holiness constrain you to sing. You are His saints chosen, blood-bought, called, and set apart for God; sanctified on purpose that you should offer the daily sacrifice of praise.*[126]

Praise is not comely from unpardoned professional singers; it is like a jewel of gold in a swine's snout. Crooked hearts make crooked music, but the upright are the Lord's delight.[127]

The Psalmist sent out a clarion call to the saved of earth to join in songs of praise to the Lord: "O come, let us sing unto the Lord: let us make a joyful noise to the Rock of our salvation."[128]

Again and again the question arises in connection with singing (as with other expressions of worship), "Is the heart in it?"

The gods of Greece and Rome may be worshipped well enough with classical music, but Jehovah can only be adored with the heart, and that music is the best for His service which gives the heart most play.[129] *We never sing so well as when we know that we have an interest in the good things of which we sing and a relationship to the God Whom we praise.*[130]

Worshipful singing was linked with several stirring narratives both in the Old Testament and the New Testament. Hezekiah commanded the Levites to sing praise unto the Lord with the words of David, and of Asaph the seer: "And they sang praises with gladness, and they bowed their heads and worshipped."[131] A nearby passage reads, "...The Levites and the priests praised the Lord day by day, singing with loud instruments unto the Lord."[132]

Henry H. Halley, famed Bible commentator, saw the need for worshipful congregational singing in churches today:

> *The whole congregation should sing. Congregational singing has a rightful place in church services. It is the part of the service that people love most; the church's chief expression of its worship of God; the one thing, ordinarily, in all the service, that has most power over people's hearts. And it is a downright shame that it has to be shoved aside to make time for long-winded preachers who so dearly love to hear themselves talk.[133]*

> *More people would go to church, and church services would have far more power over the people, if the church leadership would give CONGREGATIONAL SINGING its rightful place in the REGULAR CHURCH SERVICES, so that the people could feel that they were going to church to worship and Praise God, and not just to hear somebody preach, or sing.[134]*

These were the only personal convictions Halley expressed in his entire volume of 648 pages; hence they were his strong convictions.

This congregational singing was viewed by the United Free Church of Scotland as an occasion for the offering of praise to God. Thus the worship of God was given a prominent place in the order of service in Chart of the appendix, allowing for an effective movement of praise even in a highly ritualized service.

(2) Prayer and Praise

Not all prayer is praise; but prayer is often the vehicle upon which praise travels to its heavenly destination. The prayer of Jehoshaphat was full of praise to God when he heard that the enemy was preparing for battle. He called the people together for a season of prayer, a portion of which reads:

> *O Jehovah, the God of our fathers, art not thou God in heaven? and art not thou ruler over all the kingdoms of the nations? and in thy hand is power and might, so that none is able to withstand thee. Didst not thou, O our God, drive out the inhabitants of this land before thy people Israel, and give it to the seed of Abraham thy friend for ever?*[135]

When Paul and Silas were imprisoned at Philippi, they praised the Lord Jesus with both praying and the singing of hymns in the hearing of the prisoners.[136] The hour of midnight was in keeping with Paul's own admonition to "pray without ceasing."[137]

(3) Testimony and Praise

A regular practice in many churches has been the allowing of adherents to rise and address the audience in order to give an expression of praise to God. These are sometimes called "testimony times" or "praise services" and may be conducted at mid-week on Bible study or Prayer Meeting night, or on Sunday evening. The leader of worship often reminds the people that these testimonies properly give the "glory to the Lord" and not to the individual who testifies. Testimony time in the public service provides a time when Christians can "rejoice with them that do rejoice, and weep with them that weep."[138]

Testimonies, of course, are not limited to the church service. The Christian believer has opportunities to witness for Christ on the job, at a business meeting, on a camping trip with friends, while playing golf or while fishing, just to name a few. He or she may be riding on a train or seated with others at a luncheon. Personal testimony accompanied by an exemplary Christian life will be most effective in bringing praise to the Lord.[139]

(4) Shouting and Praise

The Psalmist approved of the loudness of praise and gave

advice to worshipers to "shout unto God with the voice of triumph."[140] This expression obviously requires an increase in volume and is in contrast to the "well-bred whispers" which Spurgeon detested:

> *Heartiness should be conspicuous in divine worship. Well-bred whis-*
> *pers are disreputable here. It is not that the Lord cannot hear us, but*
> *that it is natural for great exultation to express itself in the loudest*
> *manner. Men shout at the sight of their kings: shall we offer no loud*
> *hosannas to the Son of David?*[141]

It might be said that the shouting of praise was more spontaneous than pre-meditated. It should be kept in mind, however, that praise, in its truly biblical context, cannot engage the lips without support from the heart!

Instrumental Praise

"All kinds of musick" was acceptable for praising the Lord in Old Testament times. While I found no authority to state how many different musical instruments were in use for purposes of worship in those early days, fourteen instruments of praise were named in our Bible:

1. cornets	8. pipes
2. cymbals	9. psalteries
3. dulcimers	10. sackbuts
4. flutes	11. tabrets
5. harps	12. timbrels
6. instrument of ten strings	13. trumpets
7. organs	14. viols

In the use of these musical instruments, every faculty was enlisted in the praising of God. Wordsworth observed that:

> *The breath is employed in blowing the trumpet; the fingers are used in*
> *striking the strings of the psaltery and the harp; the whole hand is*
> *exerted in beating the timbrel; the feet move in the dance; there are*
> *stringed instruments (literally strings); there is the organ (the 'ugab,*
> *syrinx') composed of many pipes, implying combination, and the*
> *symbals clang upon one another.*[142]

Andrew Bonar tells of those who used some of these and

76

other early instruments, quoting from Patrick:

> *Patrick has an interesting note on the many instruments of music in*
> *Psalm 149, which we quote here: 'The ancient inhabitants of Etruria*
> *used the trumpet; the Arcadians, the whistle; the Sicilians, the pectid;*
> *the Cretians, the harp; the Tracians, the cornet; the Lacedemonians,*
> *the pipe; the Egyptians, the drum; the Arabians, the cymbal (Clem.*
> *Paedag., ii:4). May we not say that in this Psalm's enumeration of*
> *musical instruments, there is a reference to the variety which exists*
> *among men in the mode of expressing joy and exciting to feeling?'*[143]

Expressions which praise has taken issued occasionally in Scripture from a combination of vocal and instrumental modes. When God filled the heart with praise He put a new song in the mouth.[144] The Psalms furnish the chief evidence for this in the Old Testament. The praises of Israel were joyful outbursts in which song was mingled with shouting and dancing to a rude accompaniment of timbrels and trumpets.[145] Higher moods of praise have been expressed in the New Testament also in bursts of song.[146]

Silent Praise

Did praise always have an **audible** expression? or even necessarily something physical? It seems that God can gather up the fragments of a "broken spirit" and be glorified thereby.[147] Job, for example, worshipped God after he had "rent his robe, and shaved his head, and fell down upon the ground."[148] Of Job's experience, Helen Strong concluded:

> *Not with the voice of song, high-sounding cymbals, and the harp did*
> *Job bless God, but with rent robe and face low in the dust. The music of*
> *the world may jar the wounded, stricken heart; but in the soul the*
> *melody of praise has touched a richer, minor chord.*[149]

There is, therefore, a kind of praise which is inaudible, and Dr. Wiley's limited definition of praise was too narrow.[150] Silent praise may be considered as "praise in secret" in contrast to "praise in society" whose expressions are better known. If what you are is more important than what you have or what you do, praise offered to God has here a good maxim.

To say that praise need not be audible for God to hear brings to mind a grace before a meal given by a small daughter at the invitation of her dad. When she finished the simple prayer, she looked up, smiling, anxiously awaiting some evaluation from her father. "That was a nice prayer, honey, but I couldn't hear some of it," her dad said. "I wasn't talking to you, daddy. I was talking to God!"

Surely there are other silent forms of praise, too! Good works clearly present an additional manner in which the believer may express his praise to the Lord. Since praise was found to be from the heart, its quality depends upon the uprightness of the heart of the worshiper. C. S. Lewis's definition pointed to these moral involvements and the ethical implications of the term "praise."[151] In other words, if without holiness no man shall see the Lord;[152] without sanctification does anyone truly praise Him? What are we saying? Is it not possible that man's total relationship with God is beneath, above and beyond the mere form which his expressions of praise take?

Of course, such a view of silent praise widens its base to include such other matters as:

(a) one's position with regard to *the will of God*
(b) one's position with regard to personal stewardship
(c) one's position with regard to *the more excellent way of love*

To admit that additions could be made to this list "ad infinitum" would be to agree that the degree in which the Christian believer communicates effective, meaningful, substantial *praise to God* is contingent upon the extent to which he has already come under the approval of God. But an exhaustive list would hardly be possible. It culminates in motivation, the clearest presentation of which Paul gave to the Colossians. Paul not only sums up the whole matter, but his exhortation seems to me to be the AMEN which we need to this chapter:

> *Servants, obey in all things them that are your masters according to*
> *the flesh; not with eyeservice, as men-pleasers, but in singleness of*
> *heart, fearing the Lord: whatsoever ye do, work heartily, as unto the*

Lord, and not unto men; knowing that from the Lord ye shall receive the recompense of the inheritance: ye serve the Lord Christ.[153]

8

The Relevance
Of Praise

"...Worthy is the Lamb that was slain
to receive power, and riches, and wisdom,
and strength, and honour, and glory, and blessing."
- Rev. 5:12, KJV

Praise is both corporate and private, done in a group at worship and achieved by individuals in the closet of meditation. The latter is personal, very subjective. In this chapter, I will tell you what style or forms of worship which I have found effective to win and raise the spirits of servicemen and women, the elements of praise which I have encouraged in public worship and some of the more useful instruments and music heard in the military environment. Finally, I will expose my own preference within the context of personal praise and how I reached such conclusions.

There is no drawing power in the local church which can compare with vibrant worship services with anointed preaching and singing, with ample time reserved for praise and testimony. As a layman going to a church for the first time, if

81

all I find is cold liturgy, my heart cries out for something more. Jesus is alive. God is not dead! I just came to praise the Lord. Give me the chance to pay some of my heavy debt of thanks and praise which I owe to my Maker!

It is no different in the military setting. A church is a church, even if you call it a chapel or refer to it by some other name. If two or three of you are assembled together for an upward look in the Name of Jesus Christ, the Son of God, you have access to the throne of mercy and grace.

At this point, I feel it would be important to remind the reader that there are no free lance chaplains on active duty in any of the U. S. armed forces. Each chaplain has been ordained and endorsed for service by his denomination. He does not perform his clerical duties without deference to authority. Within the church of my ordination, the Assemblies of God, we have our own Commission on Chaplains, very ably coordinated since 1983 by Lemuel D. McElyea, and chaired by Dr. G. Raymond Carlson, General Superintendent. The Chaplaincy Department oversees the activities of 101 Army, Navy and Air Force chaplains currently on active duty, compared to 25 active military chaplains in 1963.

We ministers bring to our worship services a style of leadership borne out of cumulative experiences, observations and doctrinal beliefs. I try to adapt my style of leading a worship service to the setting which is at hand. You will appreciate the fact that years of ministering to the deaf absorbed in silence have taught me that heartfelt praise in worship need not be measured in decibels. I dearly love the old hymns of worship and find that favorites such as *A Mighty Fortress* and *The Old Rugged Cross* enhance the praises of the congregation no matter where we serve.

A little humor is helpful, of course. I broke the ice during my first visit to minister to prisoners at the Navy brig at the Navy Supply Depot in Seattle by telling this story: A sailor on leave after boot camp met an old friend in his hometown.

"How's your wife getting along?" the sailor asked.

"Guess you didn't hear...she's in heaven now," his friend replied.

"Oh, I'm sorry to hear that!" (Then, realizing he could improve on his response, the sailor quickly changed it.) "What I mean is...I'm glad to hear that!" Still not satisfied with his own response, the sailor blurted out, "What I meant to say was...I really am surprised!"

Riding piggyback on the story, I looked in the faces of thirty-some prisoners who came to hear the new brig chaplain and made the application:

"Meeting with you here in the brig like this, I must say that *I'm sorry to find out that you are here!* On the other hand, I love to point men to Christ and the more that come to a worship service like this, the better I like it. In that sense, *I'm glad to see you are here.* However, if I knew your background the way our God knows and understands...maybe I'd say 'I really am surprised to see you in the brig.'"

Those who minister in jails must constantly remember that Jesus came not to call the righteous, but sinners to repentance. (Matt. 9:13)

I have found that the preached Word under the anointing of the Holy Spirit will not return void. Also men do make eternal decisions if they are given an invitation or opportunity. Our form of worship must not deny God's power to lead men to do an about face and begin a new life in Christ. No liturgy or program will substitute for the heart-searching work of the Holy Spirit. With this fact influencing our plans to praise and worship, it becomes less a matter of our doing and more of allowing God to do His good work of leading men to repentance. I generally read from the Scriptures, invoke God's blessing upon the service, lead in the singing of hymns, and emphasize prayer on behalf of any need or problem to be solved. Special music is arranged in advance if possible.

While serving as chaplain at the Naval Training Center in San Diego, I was fortunate in being assigned to the South Chapel. Since as many as 16,000 recruits were aboard at the time, voluntary attendance on Sunday evenings ran several hundred young sailors. I could always count on dozens of decisions for Christ as a result of giving an invitation (altar call) at the conclusion of the worship hour. This assignment afforded greater opportunity for evangelism than any other place I served in the military milieu.

It has been my privilege to lead worship services at hotels in the Waikiki area of Hawaii at the invitation of Dr. Hermon S. Ray, nicknamed "the Chaplain of Waikiki." This has become almost an annual experience as I have missed only two of the last seven years to visit Oahu in wintertime. Each time Chaplain Ray puts me to work in a few of the hotels such as the Waikikian, the Napualani, Park Shore, Halekulani and Royal Hawaiian.

Encouraging praises to God in this beautiful tropical island setting is as natural as breathing. The awesome scenery, the sound of the surf, the smell of plumeria. Everything speaks to me of the work of God's hands! It's a brief service of about a half hour. But they are exciting, planned as they are by Hermon and Rayberta Ray, founders of the *Aloha Chapel Ministries*. A folding organ is often all the accompaniment needed. An accordian, guitar or ukelele can add much to set the tone for singing. Those who attend may be vacationing or locals. Find one with a fresh testimony and you will have a varied service with spontaneity. If it's just before Christmas (as it often was for me), selected carols are in order. Imagine singing, *O Come Let us Adore Him* in the Banyan Court of the Waikikian! What a wonderful Creator we have indeed! Worthy of our praise!

Most military chapels have an electric organ. Often this is all of the accompaniment necessary. Instrumental specials given by those who have the talent were encouraged, when available. A folding organ may be the only accompaniment available in remote areas or distant fields of service. No problem. You use what's at hand. The men understand. And certainly God understands!

A service chapel welcomes people from many different churches, whose hearts respond to many different styles of worship. Shall the chaplain try to "be all things to all men," alternating between the folksy style of Oklahoma Baptists and intoning the Book of Common Prayer like a high-church Episcopalian? I felt that such a changeable vesture of praise was impossible for me. I would have been insincere. I resolved to express my faith in the manner most meaningful to me, and trust the Holy Spirit to make it meaningful to military personnel and their dependents.

Men and women in the military are not that much different from the civilians back home. They want to sing praises to God in much the same way they did in their home church. Soon they realize that the beauties of stained glass windows, organs and choirs are absent from all except the largest military chapels. The refinements of praise such as a noble sanctuary may offer are seldom found near the front lines of battle. But neither God nor man expects it. Praise must come from the heart and the spirit of a man! (When Paul and Silas sang praises to God, they did so from a prison. It was no prison chapel adorned with etched windows either! Yet the power of God was there...an earthquake shook the foundations of the prison!)

Permit me to address young Christians on the importance of praising God in our daily living. But I will not here support my personal preferences with much Scripture, since that was my aim in the previous chapter. It's my testimony I want to give on the subject of praise.

I learned from the Word that Almighty God rallied on behalf of men and armies who praised Him. The Lord not only brought them victory, but He called the battle His and not man's! I learned also from the Word that it's possible to have a burden of prayer only to discover that the right words to express that burden do not seem to come. At times like these, the Holy Spirit is willing to help our weak sentences as only He can do.

Like prayer and thanksgiving, praise ought to be a constant affair. It's prayer *without ceasing*. It's *in everything* we need to give thanks. And I should bless the Lord *at all times*, with His praise *continually in my mouth*. Praise should become an on-going addiction, a habit which becomes second nature, sealed in stone.

Every child of God knows that the Lord inhabits the praises of His people. But how many are aware of the tremendous potential in terms of power to be overcomers? I have

85

come to believe that certain spiritual battles are destined for victory for those who take the time to sing out praises to God!

I do not believe that speaking in tongues was a phenomenon of the first century church which afterward disappeared. I practice waiting quietly before the Lord, in thankful remembrance for His goodness, sending Him praises in English, in Japanese or in some other tongue (unknown to me). At such times, I will be filled with the Holy Spirit with the accompanying joy as found in some experiences recorded in *The Book of Acts.*

Earlier I pointed out the constant nature of prayer, thanks and praise. There is a kinship among these three. You might add joy. Imagine any of the three without joy! I'm not talking about a short-lived "happiness" such as one might get with the news of a pay raise. This is the deep-seated, satisfying joy that earthly drugs can't produce. If you will permit me, it's getting high on Jesus!

Around the world today, the Pentecostal message is receiving wide acceptance among new believers. The Lord is adding to His church the names of those who call upon Him! Reports of revival fires in third world nations are many.

I wish I could tell you that I had discovered a simple formula for ensuring that the elements of praise are not neglected in our daily lives. As I look at what God has done by His mighty hand, especially in sending His only begotten Son to die for us, I can only conclude He does not receive enough thanks and praise from His children. As for me, so conspicuously blessed with His mercy, abundance and benefits (and so obviously undeserving!), I feel way behind on the payments I owe on my debt of praise. I find myself looking up often into the sky and soliloquizing: *"Oh, Lord, how great Thou art. For Thine is the kingdom, and the power, and the glory! Amen."*

The Book of Psalms abounds with inspiring ideas concerning praising the Lord. I am partial to passages found in Psalm 1, 19, 23, 29, 30, 34, 51, 59, 89, 91, 92, 96, 126, 148, 149 and 150.

I also dearly love the choice benediction, full of praise, found at the close of the Epistle of Jude:

"Now unto him that is able to keep you from falling, and to present you faultless before the presence of his glory with exceeding joy, To the only wise God our Saviour, be glory and majesty, dominion and power, both now and ever. Amen."

9

Now
Hear This!

My son, if thou wilt receive my words, and ...incline thine ear
unto wisdom,....Then shalt thou understand the fear of the Lord,
and find the knowledge of God."
- Proverbs 2:1, 2, 5, KJV

It's time to listen to the preacher.

If you are a high school junior or senior, this chapter is for you. Why? Because that's when the author faced the really big question: What shall I do with my life?

Never mind looking for an escape hatch. Life is too precious for you to throw it away on second best!

You have certain God-given talents. We all do. Do not permit any excuse to stand in your way from being all that you can be. Sounds like preaching? Yes, you're right. What did you expect in an autobiography of a preacher?

Life is to Enjoy!

Listen carefully. God did not put us on planet earth to fight and fuss, to step on others on the way to the top, or to get

89

high on drugs. He meant for us to learn, to smell the roses, to enjoy the sunset, to love and be loved. There's adventure for the taking. It's not too early to claim your share.

First and foremost along the path to getting the most out of life is to make your peace with God. This should not be difficult if you will act on His promise, *"Draw nigh to God, and he will draw nigh to you. Resist the devil, and he will flee from you.'*[154]

Call it getting religion if you like. The emphasis is upon a personal meeting with your heavenly Father in the quietness of meditation through His Son, Jesus Christ. You weren't given a place in this world just to get by. Life isn't worth living without Him, and in Him can be found both abundant life for earth and eternal life for heaven.

It is perfectly fitting to give yourself away in some form of service to your heavenly Father. In a recent sermon based upon the Parable of the Talents, Pastor Sam Benson said, "The person with the one talent made God mad," (not because he had only one talent, but because he buried it.) After explaining that we ought to give to God the very best performance we can possible give, Pastor Benson added, 'In the beginning, what you are is God's gift to you, but in the end, what you did is *your gift to God.*[155]

Money isn't Everything!

You are going to need money, of course. Maybe not as much of it as you think. Lots of money and a full life do not necessarily equate.

It is a mistake to accept second best in our vocational pursuits by putting money ahead of talent or desire to serve others. Consider setting out to do what you think you would really love to do and what you seem to have an aptitude for. The money will generally follow you. The emphasis here is upon discovering what you are good at, finding just what it is that you enjoy working at. Why go through life working a 9 to 5 job that is as distasteful as castor oil? What's your *real talent?*

Now that may sound like a big order. Here's a suggestion. Make it a specific matter of prayer. Team up with God.

With your heavenly Father leading the way, get up off your knees...and get going! There's a big world out there. You have lots to do. What a wonderful time you will have in the pursuit of happiness...your's and His! Remember, you want to please God in all of life's endeavors.

How much Education is Enough?

The question itself is wrong. We never stop learning.

While the classroom is a good place to learn, it's merely one place. You will find that life will be richer and fuller if you develop the habit of learning wherever you go. At home, in the library, at church, on a trip. You should become knowledgeable as you mature, but it's not a worthwhile end in itself. Formal classroom education will get you academic degrees. These may or may not be what you need, however. Obviously, your chosen profession will dictate. Have you looked at the cost of college tuition lately? It's enough to make you want to look in any direction other than being a teacher! On the other hand, if you think education is expensive, try ignorance.

Suppose you have a mechanical aptitude? You will be looking for a hands-on technical institute. If this is your talent and you feel that it will open the door to a fine opportunity for you, by all means go for it. An advanced degree will not be required in such circumstances. This can be an advantage since you will enter the job market long before your contemporaries who opt for a profession requiring years of classroom studies. The emphasis here will be to avoid the expensive halls of learning unless they will contribute to your vocational goals.

What about Love and Marriage?

"If the Navy wanted you to have a wife, it would have issued you one!" The author heard that line first at the Naval Training Center in San Diego, but it might just as easily have originated from some Marine sergeant at Camp Pendleton. We can all chuckle at a quip like that one, but marriage is not receiving top billing these days.

Matrimony was intended by God to be a holy union of

marriage between a man and a woman. Marriage was God's first institution for the welfare of the race. This occurred centuries ago in the Garden of Eden. Heavenly hosts witnessed the wonderful scene as God established the rite of marriage!

It may sound trite to hear another preacher point out that unless God blesses your marital union, you should not expect optimum joy and blessings of love and marriage. Family values begin with the sanctity of the marriage vows. Any other arrangement falls short of God's best for you! It is significant that Jesus performed his first recorded miracle at Cana in Galilee at a marriage feast.[156]

Why not Give Yourself Away?

While you are giving serious thought to your long range plans for this life, may I remind you of the ancient concept of service. This is the idea that there is a great sense of satisfaction in serving others. You may recall the words of the Lord Jesus, *"It is more blessed to give than to receive."*[157] Closely akin to this is the notion of finding one's life by losing it.[158] Jesus told his disciples that true greatness would be found in a position of service.[159]

Quite obviously, Jesus was making a good case for spending one's life by denying self, following Him, and working for the good of the kingdom of God.

In a broader sense, however, many individuals have "found themselves" by giving up normal lives to serve humanity. Inventors such as Jonas Salk, Thomas Edison and Alexander Graham Bell are among those whose patience and dedication changed our lives. Some American presidents deserve to be classified as servants of the people in a broad sense of the term. How about Abraham Lincoln or Franklin Delano Roosevelt?

So many roads to choose! Each of us has only one life. To make the most of it is a natural desire. Consider the *attitude* of service whether you select waiting tables or loaning money, raising cattle or building houses, architecture or optometry. In America there is room for all. And all are needed!

Speaking of America, have you thought much about the

so-called "American Dream?" What does it mean to you? Some think of it in terms of owning a home. In America, this dream can come true. Start saving!

Whatever the American Dream means to you, it pays to dream. Dreams have a way of sparking some worthy goals in our lives. But it's not enough to merely dream! Your dream to become a reality will require, more than any thing else, a decision to act. The riddle of three frogs will illustrate:

> *Once upon a time there were three frogs sitting on a lily pad. One of these little frogs decided to jump. Now how many are left? the riddle asks. Your answer? Two? No, Three, because he only "decided" that he would jump. Your noblest dreams will remain merely dreams until you get off the pad and make the jump. Get off the pad!*

Are You Looking After Your Soul?

Body, soul and spirit, three components. That's us! But we spend far more on the body than we spend on soul or spirit. The body must have food, clothes, dental care, shampoo, and plenty of soap. For starters. What's the one important thing you need to get for your soul? A Bible![160] Jesus confronted his disciples with the previously mentioned quality of life followed by the relative value of the soul:[161]

> *"If you insist on saving your life, you will lose it. Only those who throw away their lives for my sake and for the sake of the Good News will ever know what it means to really live.*
>
> *"And how does a man benefit if he gains the whole world and loses his soul in the process? For is anything worth more than his soul?"*

We all understand that the body needs food. But the soul needs food, too! And food for the soul comes right out of the written Word of God. When Jesus was very hungry after forty days of fasting, the devil wanted Him to prove He was the Son of God by commanding that stones be made bread. Jesus replied:[162]

> *"It is written, Man shall not live by bread alone, but by every word that proceedeth out of the mouth of God."*

Where will you find such words from the mouth of God?

93

In the Holy Bible, that's where! The author recommends that you take your time, shop around, and get a good one. Which version? You might wish to discuss this with a good Bible preacher. King James is fine. So is the New King James version. Get them all if you like. This is for your *soul*. (How many outfits (suits/dresses) do you have for the body?) And which is more valuable, the body or the soul? You remembered, didn't you?!

Are You Taking Good Care of Your Body?

To be sure, the soul is more valuable than the body. Nevertheless, the one body you were given is the only one you're going to get. Taking care of it is no small feat! Big feet? Well, not that. Good health is not something we should be careless about.

The importance of eating right, getting plenty of exercise and enough sleep cannot be over-emphasized. Of course, this is only a start. Staying off drugs, tobacco and booze, (Oh, preacher, I thought you'd get around to that!) Anything that is harmful to the body is taboo if you are serious about being at your best for life.

Dress for success? Here's a better idea: Dress for comfort. Don't wear shoes that do not fit! In a word, take care of yourself. You are very important: to your parents, to your friends, to your God...and very important to yourself!

By all means, learn to like yourself. When you look in the mirror what do you see? In your youth you have it all. Good looks, health, a whole life of opportunity out there just waiting for you. Looking for open doors! In a way, a closed door is better. Why? Because you don't have to decide whether to enter or not! (Unless, of course, you insist on prying it open, which could be a big mistake).

Sure, we're all so different from one another. All races, creeds, nationalities. We must make a conscious effort to respect each other, to love and pray for each other. That's Christ's way. It's a good way...the best.

Go for Broke

Which do you consider better? To set a medium goal of attainment or to set a high goal of attainment? (If you respond

94

by denying the value of goal-setting, we need to talk!) When God created the heaven and the earth, the sun, moon and stars, He did so by using His mind and His spoken word. It is noteworthy that He *turned to Himself* when He created man. He said "Let us make man in our image." (Genesis 1:26) This can only mean that you have powers of creativity resident in your mind and words, too! If God made you, and made you in His own image, it follows that you should aim to employ some of that creativity in life. We are not limiting ourselves to sons and daughters here. This capability God gave us to create human life is marvelous indeed! But God had a good time making things out of nothing. And if you think it's impossible for a person like yourself to accomplish the same thing, read the eleventh chapter of the epistle to the Hebrews, which contains not only a concise definition of *faith*, but more than a dozen examples of men and women who used their faith to please God.

Decide what you want to create. A business? A large construction company? A life of government service? A life of missionary service? Go for broke! Be the best you can be. Set your goal at the top. Mediocrity isn't good enough for you! Believe that you are better than that. Have faith in yourself. Ask God for wisdom to triumph, to march all of the way through to victory! Set your goal high. You'll reach it!

Try Feather-touch Control

What have we learned from the computer age that can help us in our daily chores? If nothing else, we have discovered that there is a faster method of accomplishing tasks than the cumbersome method of yesteryear. Funny thing, I learned something about this a few decades ago from Maxine Williams at Northwest College. I didn't know a computer from a cash register at the time! I was enrolled in a class in "Early Childhood Education," of all things. Miss Williams, our professor, was explaining the essentials of how to maintain control while teaching a large group of children. "Time doesn't permit you to give each child individual attention," she said. After stressing the importance of visual aids and eye contact, she said what is needed is a sort of *Feather-touch Control*. We're talking about time management, of course. Why spend hours at a task when it can be accomplished in minutes? Or in seconds? Why take a long, time-consuming route to your destination if you can discover a short-cut without sacrificing quality of the end-product? You get the idea.

Few ventures will succeed without mastery of communication skills. Fortunately, the tools for rapid and effective communication are getting plenty of attention these days. A distraught mother finally got a phone call from her college daughter and chastised her with, "Karen, where have you been? You don't call. You don't write. You don't FAX!" On the other hand, phones and FAX machines are very impersonal. If at all possible within your limitations of time, arrange a face-to-face meeting for optimum communication. The sheer volume of your work load may not afford the luxury of a personal encounter. But do it whenever the situation calls for it. Less than a one-on-one is *much less than best!*

Erase the Minus Factors

Once you have discovered your talent and have set your goals, expect plenty of dissuasions. The line forms on the right with an endless number of unsolicited "counselors" who want you to believe they have only your best interest in mind. Even close friends and relatives join the line up! Your position must be clearly fixed. Your heart must be set on some special project. You will not be fully satisfied unless you either reach the fulfillment of your dream or lay down your life trying. Here's where faith and determination must rise to the occasion. It is time to refuse to accept negative advice. I know you've heard this before in a number of ways. I call it "erasing the minus factors."

What are these minus factors? They are not always easy to recognize, sneaking into your life uninvited. They are insidious and you'll probably be tempted to welcome these minus factors at times as the solution to your temporary dilemma. That's because, more often than not, they offer an easy way out. They promise something for nothing. These obstacles in the way of your progress will not be so kind as to loom up on the road ahead with a sign that reads, DETOUR. Count on it, nevertheless. Here is a detour which may take you miles off course. Generally speaking, a minus factor is any idea or suggestion which has the power to divert you from your primary goal(s). Only you can make the big decisions along the way! Keep your dream alive by staying on course! Believe in yourself. You cannot afford to listen to the negative advice of anyone. If your goal calls for sacrifice, then be willing to *sacrifice*. If it calls for education, then *study*! If it calls for money, get it... legally. Crime? That's out! Drugs? No way! Divorce? There's a better way! Vacation? If you need one! Think it can't be done? Do it anyway!

Possibility Permeation is Positively Proper

This is not the first time you have heard that positive thinking works wonders and that lots of things are possible for us if we will only believe. You will now hear it from me, too. Thinking positively is just another example of faith operating in your life. I make no apologies for my appreciation for rock-bottom, Bible-based possibility preaching. Two of my favorite exponents are Dr. Norman Vincent Peale and Dr. Robert Schuller. I met Dr. Peale and heard him speak at the U.P.S. Fieldhouse in Tacoma. Years later I heard him again in his Marble Collegiate Church in New York. While I've not met Robert Schuller, I read his books and watch him regularly on television.

Let's get one thing straight. The Bible is a positive book. That's because Almighty God thinks positively. Boy, does that sound trite! But, how do you suppose the Creator brought all things into existence if He had a lot of doubts while the plans were still on the drawing boards? Look at just one of His major feats...human beings. Molding the heart, brain and nervous system must have been a mind-boggling project! The truth is, God was not quite finished with the job centuries ago. He *sustains* your life on a day-by-day basis! (Isn't it time you made your peace with Him?)

My preaching was filled with this <u>possibility</u> tack. Perhaps, this helps explain why God asked me to *practice* for half a lifetime the things I preached for twenty-one years. I don't know. All I know is that it has been excitement and adventure to work at being an optimist. A dozen years ago, I woke up one morning to hear that I would be awarded a Ph.D. degree. That was the same week that my accountant said my financial statement showed in excess of one million dollars net worth. I humbly thanked Jesus for these...and only eight years into *practicing*.

10

Northwest College Forever!

"Open my eyes
to see wonderful things
in your Word."
- Psalm 119:18, The Living Bible

There is something about following as God leads that makes everything turn out just right in the end. I look upon those classroom experiences at Northwest Bible College as the springboard for my life's journey. I use the word "experiences" simply because I was after the *heart-knowledge* more than the kind of head-knowledge that "puffeth up" (I Cor. 8:1, KJV). I got what I went after.

With military service behind me, I had the GI Bill. When I looked at Northwest Bible College in 1948 its enrollment had reached 376 students. While women outnumbered men by about two to one, the addition of many World War II veterans helped even the ratio of male to female. Ward Tanneberg pointed out those interesting statistics about veterans and gender ratios in his book, "Let Light Shine Out."[163] True, I was a veteran and one that needed a GI Bill to help with tuition. But the fact that female students outnumbered male students was of little consequence to me. That's because Donna and I got married during the first month of my four-year college work. That was something that required special permission from the school, but I will spare you the details!

Speaking of being married while in Bible college, my close and dear friend, John Simpson, remained single those four years. We couldn't know it then, but he became an Army chaplain, retiring with the grade of colonel.

I needed to work hard to support my growing family. During the four years, I held four jobs, all in Seattle: Thompson Candy House, Firland Sanatorium, Attorney's Messenger Service and Northgate Brokers. After the arrival of our first daughter, Beverly, Donna chose to stay home to be the mother rather than attempt to work outside the home. We both felt that children need a mother while growing up. God never failed to meet our financial needs since we knew how to be thrifty. Study and work kept us busy. We were happy indeed!

In those days, Northwest Bible College was located in Seattle. The college moved to a new 35-acre campus in Houghton, now Kirkland, in 1959, the same year its name was changed to *Northwest College*. Interstate 5 freeway now passes directly over the site of the old institution. Those early alums will have to look hard to find their "roots" under that slab of concrete!

Thanks be to God, I was not finished with NC...nor was NC finished with me.

I had not been out of the Navy a week when President D. V. Hurst called me with an invitation to join the college's staff to fill a vacancy left when Reverend Ward Tanneberg resigned as Director of Public Relations.

We were still unpacking boxes in our Puyallup home when the call was taken. I told Dr. Hurst that I would like to think about it and pray about it before making a decision. Then, after a brief pause, I squeezed the phone a little harder and said, "I've thought about it enough and prayed about it, and can come to Kirkland to discuss details Monday, if you like." That was the beginning of learning more through Northwest College from a much different perspective. It would also afford a splendid transition from Navy life to civilian life. Furthermore, perhaps this will allow time for me to discover what God meant when He said, "Practice what you preached."

The PR job turned out to be a real challenge. When I heard the names of some of the men who held the position, I wondered if I could measure up: B. P. Berkeland, Herb Crowder, Warren Bullock, Ward Tanneberg!

Among the interesting duties of the PR job was the preparation of the annual itinerary for the two college choral groups. One was a full choir of about thirty-one voices and the other an ensemble of nineteen voices. Suggested dates were offered to regional church pastors. This was all a part of student recruitment. For the student participants, it was a great experience, too. Relationships formed were priceless! The college's energetic music director, Dr. W. R. Swaffield, was truly fun to work with. Donna and I formed a lasting, warm friendship with Bob and Phyllis Swaffield.

It was my privilege also to travel with one of the choirs. At times, I accompanied the so-called PR teams, singing groups composed of four or five students. These were a good introduction to ministry for students, a fun thing to do, and certainly a mutual benefit between the churches and the college.

Typically, the choir would arrive at the church early enough for a few minutes quiet time before changing for the Sunday evening service. While at Bethany Christian Assembly in Everett, Washington, I stretched out on a pew "for some meditation." Well, that was a mistake! Soon I was snoring. (I wish I could deny it, but the evidence was right there for all to hear!) One of the tenors put a microphone to my mouth and recorded the loudest snort you ever heard. The fun part (for the choir!) came when, as a total surprise to their incredulous PR man, one of the men announced: "Now, we will hear a few remarks from our Public Relations Director, Reverend Ron DeBock..." With that he turned the switch on the tape recorder. I can't tell you how much I laughed. Who was it that said, "You only hurt the ones you love!?"

The PR job at NC gave me just the breather I needed. It was sort of a bridge over the river "Why?" and gave me time to find out why I received those intriguing, divine orders, *"Practice what you preached."*

There is an understandable sense of satisfaction for anyone fortunate enough to be involved in training young people in an institution such as Northwest College. Perhaps it is a sense of eternal values, that there is something going on which will truly count—not for this life only, but for eternity. Members of the faculty and administration are, therefore, fun to work with. They are a happy lot. One can feel that these are servants of the Lord, with "a calling" to the important task of Christian higher education. Believe me, such endeavor is truly a high calling.

The 35-acre campus acquired by President Charles Butterfield in 1958 had grown to about 45 acres by the time I came aboard in 1971, due to the college's acquisition of contiguous parcels. Overlooking Lake Washington to the west, NC's campus was widely acknowledged to be the most beautiful of all the denomination's regional colleges. (When the Seattle Seahawks leased the southeast portion of NC's campus for a training camp, it gave the campus a further boost of identity!)

One of my responsibilities was to show off this campus to visitors. Moms, dads, prospective students and others wanted to see the dormitories, the library, the chapel, the cafeteria and classrooms. One prospective student had it all figured out when he saw the human skeleton in biology lab: "Is this fellow a victim of eating in the college cafeteria?"

On moving to Kirkland, we bought a modest home near the college on good terms. It was a fine home within walking distance to campus. We were comfortable in the Kirkland residence and entertained faculty and others occasionally.

Donna and I invited guests to our Silver Wedding Anniversary while in that home. One of the couples who came was Phil and Roberta Gustafson. A close and dear friend, Phil was at the time a mathematics professor. I happened to overhear

Phil ask our oldest daughter, Beverly, her age. "I'm twenty-six," Bev replied without a telltale expression to indicate she was fibbing. For a satisfying moment at least, we watched Phil swallow and plot his next move. To the relief of saints, Beverly finally corrected her age to "twenty-four next December."

Ronald and Dean

Ronnie

Donna, Bev and Ronald

*Ron and Donna with Gary,
Bev and Jan*

*Donna June Walsworth
Puyallup High Grad
Class of 1949*

*Ron, Donna and "crew"
during seminary days*

105

Bev, Japan's poster girl

The Richardsons (left to right) John, Nellie,
Leslie, Dennis, Ira, Charlie, Ted, Ned (Ron's dad) and Fred

*Ron in '64
at NAS, Memphis*

Gus and Olive DeBock with Bev

Angela Satter, Bev's oldest girl   *Ashley Satter, Bev's youngest*

"… houses will gather to you"

Gary at 5th and West Main

Puyallup First Assembly of God

Puyallup Development Center

Holy Land Tour in '85

Ron on Mt. Sinai

Gary DeBock marries Ruth in Hong Kong

11

What Did
He Practice?

"And those who are peacemakers
will plant seeds of peace
and reap a harvest of goodness."
- James 3:18 , TLB

How does a man of the cloth rationalize a complete change
of careers? Is there any way a minister of the Gospel can
justify leaving the ministry for mammon?

Funny thing, when Reverend R. G. DeBock resigned the
pastorates at Lakebay and Longbranch Community Churches
to take graduate work to prepare for the Navy chaplaincy at
age 28, a lady in one of the churches said, "Our minister is
leaving the ministry to join the Navy!"

It is no small feat for the minister of any denomination to
qualify for orders to active duty as a military chaplain in any
branch of the United States armed forces. He must be a college
graduate and a graduate of an approved theological seminary. He (or *she* now!) must be an ordained member with an
ecclesiastical endorsement from his church denomination for

115

the purpose of active duty in a particular branch of military service. He must also meet strict age and physical requirements.

Were it not for the fact that Chaplain DeBock had sustained such a hearing loss while serving on active duty in the U. S. Naval Reserve, there would be no need to actually *change careers*. He might have made himself available to serve as the pastor of a local church, for example. However, the hearing impairment was substantial enough to disqualify Ron for a pulpit.

Besides, the clear voice of God was still ringing in his ears, and did make a lot of sense the more Ron thought about the matter of a new vocation. How much easier it would have been for Ron if God had just narrowed it down a bit: *"Now, hear this...sell real estate!"* But, He didn't. God made human beings in His own image. This means that, like God, we are to make our own choices in life. The choices that are the most important include a spouse and a career. These follow after the choice for eternity in the light of the fate that awaits all flesh. (See Hebrews 9:27)

So, what would Ron practice? Given the pragmatic individual that he is, Ron looked over the facts. What did he have left after you take away excellent hearing? What was he looking for? What education would any new vocation require? At age 43, is it too late to start over? And, taking a line that came right out of the Bible, what did he have in the house? (See II Kings 4:2) How would his family get involved, if at all? It's hard enough to commence at commencement (as from college). But, try starting the process all over again after going down one road for more than two decades!

At about the same time that DeBock was being separated from the Navy, a billboard in the Seattle area was to become famous as a harbinger of days ahead, *"Will the last one out of Seattle please turn off the lights?"* The early seventies brought to the Northwest depression and unemployment.

Back at the Naval Training Center in Great Lakes, Illinois, a disbursing officer handed Ron a check for slightly over $11,000 as severance pay. He explained to the former chaplain that he was receiving the maximum of $15,000, but the taxes were being withheld. "Just sign here, and you're on your way," he said.

"There must be some mistake," Ron said. "Do you know about the change in medical separation pay effective last November?"

"Let me see that check, sir! You are absolutely right. There should be no tax withheld either!" he said. "Come back after 2:00 p.m. and another check will be ready."

Another lieutenant commander in the Chaplain Corps had also received his separation pay of somewhat more than $11,000 after taxes at the same facility. (Ron had heard of him, but had never met him). Someone asked the other chaplain what he planned to do with his separation money. As the story goes, he would buy a house in Georgia).

That same afternoon Chaplain DeBock picked up a revised check for well over $31,000 tax free. "That's closer to what I figured," Ron said with a smile.

"What will you do with all that money? Buy a new home like Chaplain John Doe?"(not his real name as if you didn't guess), a nearby well-wisher asked. It was the first time Ron had given the matter a serious thought. But his reply was undoubtedly something of a surprise.

"No, I don't need any more houses. I already have 13 of them and I plan to live in one of them in beautiful Puyallup." Until now, Ron had been reticent concerning the accumulation of rental houses. He seldom mentioned them. Then he realized that he failed to mention the St. Helens Apartments or the five acres he and Donna purchased within the year. Oh well, what's the difference? This is not an auditor or C.P.A.! (Besides, Ron was just a poor preacher, wasn't he?) Then Ron recalled a story he used to tell:

A new minister at the local church took his car to the shop for repair. While negotiating the price with the mechanic, the minister seemed relieved that it would cost just $50.00.

"I'm just a poor preacher, you know." the new pastor said.

"Yes, I know. I heard you last Sunday!" replied the mechanic.

What did Ron practice? Well, for one thing, he just *knew that God was leading*. What mattered most was simply letting God lead the way. This is not to say there was no need to plan. There was! It was just that if God wants to take him the long route instead of the more direct route, that was perfectly all right.

Donna and Ron had barely unpacked the moving van in Puyallup, when an interesting job offer came via a phone call. Ron felt this was of God. The three and one-half years as Director of Public Relations at Northwest College of the Assemblies of God in Kirkland, Washington, was a challenge, exciting and a perfect transition back into *civilian life*.

Ron purchased a big two-story, ten-room house in the small town of Puyallup. He lived there for several years, but gradually remodelled the entire lower floor into office spaces. From this office, he ran a company which he started from scratch. The only employees were his bookkeeper and secretary. Later, his son, Gary, came aboard to be manager. Part-time maintenance personnel were on call to keep rental units habitable and in good repair.

The location became well-known. Foot traffic increased. Inquirers by phone would sometimes hear Ron say something like: "You can't miss us. We're on the corner of Hollywood and Vine, downtown Puyallup!" It was old, an antique, but in a central location. Donna kept the rose garden blossoming. Ron mowed the lawn. (Brighten the corner where you are!).

The time came when it was no longer necessary to live in the same house where the office was situated. After a few failed attempts to obtain a nearby residence, in 1985, the perfect solution emerged across the street a half-block from the rental office. The picturesque old antique home had been completely remodelled with lots of brick, even a brickish fence. Finally, a comfortable home to live in! They had been like the cobbler's son with no shoes to wear. (They had lots of rental houses, but none suitable, close to the work place). Ron had not prayed for this latest house either. You will enjoy hearing why he did not pray for houses!

There are two things which Ron DeBock did not pray for: (1) houses and (2) money.

Why wouldn't Ron pray for houses? He was a real estate salesman at age 23 while working his way through Bible College. At the time, he took an option on the lovely home where they lived during his senior year.

Just before graduation, Ron talked with the Lord about the option. He specifically asked that he be permitted to exercise the option and buy the home. It was in Lake City, a suburb of Seattle. (The details appear in Chapter One of this book). But the answer to Ron's prayer was:

"My son, seek my will, obey me, and houses will gather to you."

Ron took the answer as a "NO."

Nevertheless, Ron moved into a new 3-bedroom house for his first full-time pastorate. For that reason, Ron would not understand the cryptic answer to his first and only prayer for a house until many years later.

Much later, houses did indeed gather to him. In the seventies, Ron helped his son, Gary, acquire rental homes, too. Following in his dad's footsteps, Gary owned six rental houses at age 22.

Ron practiced what he preached as far as landlording goes, too. He bought dozens of houses, duplexes, a tri-plex, mobile homes and acreage. He even bought a church and parsonage!

How did Ron practice what he preached? By giving. The beauty of having possessions is that it affords a position of strength from which one can give to others and to the Lord's work. Such gifts will not be named in this book. God knows.

Navy orders came often. Sometimes every two years, but sometimes each year. Ron's habit was to buy a house practically every time they made a move. It was not difficult to do.

He would borrow three months' pay for the down payment and repay the loan (affectionately referred to as a *dead horse!*) in six months by having it withheld from his regular pay. It meant living frugally, but that was nothing new for the DeBocks. This will account for the fact that Ron was able to invest in several rental houses while on active duty. Obviously, therefore, he never prayed for houses. The one house he had prayed for (in Lake City) would never be his in the will of God, despite the option. That was the last time he asked his heavenly Father for a house. (But he didn't need to either!)

As for praying for money, the ban on saying one word to God about it was a conviction Ron had from his understanding of the Scriptures. His line of reasoning went something like this: God was his provider. It is not the money one needs, but the things money buys or cannot buy. A number of references from God's Word supported his belief:

> *"But your heavenly Father already knows perfectly well that you need them (food & clothing), and He will give them to you if you give Him first place in your life and live as He wants you to."*
> *- Matthew 6:32-33, TLB*

> *"No good thing will He withhold from those who walk along His paths."*
> *- Psalm 84:11b, TLB*

There was also the fact that God's Son humbled Himself and became poor so that anyone who believes in Him could become rich. Here was the King of kings and the Lord of lords from heaven above! The provision had already been made when God sent His Son to earth. And Jesus was obedient to the plan of redemption, all the way to the cross where a great victory was won over Satan and death itself.

> *"For ye know the grace of our Lord Jesus Christ, that, though He was rich, yet for your sakes He became poor, that ye through His poverty might be rich."*
> *- 2 Corinthians 8:9 KJV*

Then, too, DeBock had travelled to third world countries where poverty was rampant. Governments were unsuccessful in coping with widespread hunger. By comparison, America was a paradise, indeed. Ron did not feel right about a prayer for money when God had already given him all a man could ask for...a beautiful wife, a wonderful family, good health, a sound mind and a Lord Who was only too pleased to add to his conspicuous abundant living.

Finally, if Ron might have entertained a notion to pray for money, he could not do so after the year 1990. That was the year of harvest to be remembered. The years of sowing had paid off! It was not only the best year for Ron's business, but it was also the year when his only son, Gary, would take a wife. Gary was promoted to General Manager of *Rainier Rentals*. Donna and Ron went to the wedding in Hong Kong where Ruth Hui became Gary's beautiful Chinese bride. It was a good year for the DeBocks!

How did Ron practice what he had preached long ago? He lived a frugal life-style in order to plant seeds of realty investment. If it's true that a person will reap what he sows, he might consider doing some sowing early in life. Yes, education is also a seed, but Ron favored solid investing in real estate. Most of these were acquired in the vicinity where he was living at the time. A partial list of these investments follows:

Single Family Homes: One each in the Washington cities of Woodinville, Marysville, Sumner, Graham, Milton, Kirkland and Kapowsin. One in Zion, Illinois. Two in Seattle, six in Tacoma and nineteen in Puyallup, Washington.

Multiple Units: A duplex in Tacoma and a duplex in Puyallup; a tri-plex in Puyallup; an eight-plex in Puyallup.

Acreage: 14.5 acres in Graham, 5 acres in Kapowsin, 5 acres in Eatonville and 1.17 acres in Puyallup.

Miscellaneous: Five mobile home lots in Sumner and Graham with three mobile homes; a church and parsonage in Puyallup and an office building in Puyallup.

Practicing what he used to preach took an interesting new twist for Ron DeBock. He used to be in the pulpit. Now he was in the pew! How does an ordained minister function in the local church?

The last thing Ron wanted to do was get in the way of any pastor in the local Assembly of God (church) where he worshipped. He should attend and support the church of his choice, but humble himself and be a *layman*. Ron called himself a "layman with an inside track."

There are strict guidelines for ordained ministers to follow who find themselves attending a church where they hold no office on the pastoral staff. For example, district church regulations prohibit the ordained minister from being a deacon or trustee in a local church.

Ron had no qualms about where he stood, no aspirations to fill the pulpit as in times past. On the contrary, he wanted to be guided by the Master, Himself, who *"made himself of no reputation...and humbled himself and became obedient..."* (Philippians 2:5-9, NKJV). Of course, Ron was very much aware of the words of Jesus, *"For whoever exalts himself will be abased, and he who humbles himself will be exalted."* Abiding by the known teachings of Jesus and the known rules of the denomination as it pertains to its ordained clergy was all part of practicing what DeBock believed in and used to preach. Now was the time to practice it!

Which church should Reverend DeBock attend? Well, that's easy to answer. He had returned to the same little town where he graduated from high school. And while attending school, Ron also attended the Puyallup First Assembly of God. Although the church outgrew its old building, it was basically the same congregation. Here was the church where he met Donna June Walsworth, who later became his wife and most ardent supporter. Why should Ron change churches? Ron maintained his membership in that local assembly throughout his chaplaincy career. He always thought of it as a winner.

You will no doubt appreciate the fact that it was critical for Ron to have all such clerical questions answered in his heart. Was he now a real estate broker? Or was he a minister? Obviously, Ron was not the only retired minister who ever needed to resolve such issues. But, don't forget that God had told Ron to "practice what he preached." Just how would he put those former preachments into practice? He wanted to do it. He would do it!

Let's get one thing straight. God is perfectly capable of granting ordination to any person with or without the help of an earthling! Jesus made this clear when He told His disciples, *"Ye have not chosen me, but I have chosen you, and ordained you, that ye should go and bring forth fruit, and that your fruit should remain: that whatsoever ye shall ask of the Father in My name, He may give it you."* (John 15:16, KJV)

Try to put yourself in Ron's shoes for a moment. He was still ordained and proudly carried a little card in his wallet known as "Ordained Fellowship Card." For 39 years he carried such a card issued annually by the General Council of the Assemblies God with headquarters in Springfield, Missouri. Ron believed in the doctrines and enjoyed good fellowship with a host of ministers within the denomination.

Don't forget that men and women of all vocations sat in the pews when Reverend DeBock was in the pulpit. Including ministers, of course!

What might have been a dilemma was not a problem for Ron. And the reason there was no problem to be solved was because of Ron's faith in the divine guidance he received back in 1971, "Practice what you preached." In a sense, it was exactly what he had asked for as a 15-year-old high school student while at prayer in the tower of the Foursquare Church in Olympia. He figured he looked at one particular verse of Scripture more than others:

Jeremiah 33:3. *"Call upon me, and I will answer thee, and shew thee great and mighty things, which thou knowest not."*

So, what if it took twenty-eight years to get an answer to that promise? When you remember that a day is as a thousand years on one of God's calendars, that's only about an hour and one-half to wait!

A remarkable coincidence became evident at the annual congregational business meetings in the local church, too. In the late seventies, while Reverend Kenneth Woll was the senior pastor, the Puyallup church's net worth was conspicuously at the same level as Ron's own net worth appeared on his annual financial statement. A little above, a little beneath. It was so close! Ron said nothing to anyone about the coincidence, however, not even to his wife. But year after year, it became somewhat of a fascination. Since Ron was busily engaged in land investments at the time, he came to think of the coincidence as a comparison *between heaven and earth.*

One other factor added to the intrigue. In the late seventies, Ron was working on a doctorate. His doctoral dissertation was entitled, *"A Comparison Between the Financing of New Worship Facilities of the Assemblies of God and Nazarenes in Washington State."* It so happened that over the next several years, his local church would experience a devastating fire, rebuilding and phenomenal growth in attendance.

But the church also went deeply into debt. Despite his experience, studies and intense interest in the local problem, Ron remained a keen observer. Senior pastors came and went. The debt grew and became less manageable. Attempts at refinancing were kept before the congregation. Meanwhile, he was seldom privy to true financial data since his ordained status precluded a position on the Board of Trustees.

Nevertheless, please do not misunderstand the previous paragraph. At no time did Ron feel left out. He was there...an active member... ready, willing and able to lend support. More than that, his objective never changed. He was trying to practice what he once preached.

Beneath it all for Ron was a mind-boggling picture in his mind of Jesus, the Son of God, who gave up everything for mankind. Of course, this is theological...seminary stuff. But, the contemplation of the Son of God leaving heaven, coming to earth as a baby, being tempted, only to die obediently on a cross seemed so amazing and wonderful. That He would so humble Himself seemed so incredible. That He would not immediately retaliate when angels were under His command seemed marvelous. Were it not that Jesus was following the Father's great plan for the redemption of souls, none of it makes sense at all. *"For God so loved the world, that He gave His only begotten Son, that whosoever believeth in him should not perish, but have everlasting life."*[164]

Ron figured that if he was going to put into practice some of those admonitions he once gave to his own congregations, he should use his own teaching talent. Pastors are always looking for volunteer teachers, it seems. Even when regular teachers are in ample supply, alternates are always needed to relieve the regulars at relief time or during vacations.

For this reason, Ron volunteered to teach in the local assembly's "Family Life Education" department. He genuinely enjoys teaching and prepares himself with the same dedication as he did while in full-time active ministry. A few lesson notes appear in the Appendix.

12

The
Milton Miracle

*"Do not despise this
small beginning, for the eyes of the Lord
rejoice to see the work begin..."*
- Zechariah 4:10, TLB

If it's a big money-making real estate deal you'd like to read about, don't look for it in this chapter.

The little two-bedroom house which Ron bought for cash in 1974 in Milton, Washington, was the sort of deal he liked. It wasn't due to a small down payment. He paid cash for the house. But he felt the hand of God in the entire transaction from beginning to closing, and beyond.

Milton is a small town about three miles North of Puyallup, a quiet community handy to the I-5 freeway which joins Tacoma and Seattle.

Ron likes to tell a story about Milton which grew out of a vacation trip along the California coast. He stopped to browse in one of the curio shops to admire works of art. The proprietor of the burl factory was eager to expand his sales by increasing his sales outlets. Noting the Washington state license plates on Ron's car, the owner asked if he had considered opening a store where he could sell burl crafts. "We can wholesale to you."

"Come to think of it, there is a vacant building on North Meridian in Milton near my home," Ron replied. "For a business name, how does *'Milton Burl'* sound?" The rollicking owner laughed all the way to his atlas.

A little background will be helpful. Real estate prices were depressed in the Northwest back in 1974. (With hindsight it would have been a good time to invest in a rental house...or two! Ron did.)

On the day he purchased the Milton house, Ron received a phone call from a saleslady concerning the property listed for sale by her broker. (Seven months previously she sold a small house to DeBock at which time he requested that she remember him if she should ever find another low-priced house for a rental investment).

"I have a tiny house I think you should see. It's in Milton," she said. "Tell me about it!" Ron replied, "How much is it selling for?"

"The asking price is $2,700.00. It is a two-bedroom house on a big lot with apple trees. And it is selling with furniture included," she added.

"Wait a minute," Ron interrupted. "You must mean the down payment is $2,700.00?"

"No, that's the total price," the licensed saleslady insisted. Ron looked at his watch. It was 11:00 a.m.

"I'll meet you at your office at noon and we'll have a look."

While driving to Milton, DeBock wondered how any property could be for sale at such a low figure. Several questions came to mind. Where do the owners live? Why are they selling? Does such a selling price include a sales commission for the broker? What sort of furnishings are included? There must be something wrong with this place! What's wrong with it? Is it scheduled for condemnation? Or something worse? Wait and see!

To make a long story longer, this is what he found: a 704 square foot one story frame house with hardwood floors and an asphalt roof that did not leak. It was built in 1935 and was situated on a gently sloping lot which was 100' X 213' with a splendid view to the south. While county records indicated values then at $4,247 for the house and $3,075 for the land, the out of state owners were anxious to sell in order to move their elderly mother from the home.

- The house was furnished with a few notable antiques.
- The hot water tank was piped from the wood range!
- Several apple trees appeared healthy and promising of fruit.
- A coin collection contained 19 old pennies.
- An old fur stole was in the closet.
- A full-length fur coat was in the closet.
- One pair of men's shoes was in the closet.
- Dry wood for a fireplace was cut and stacked (2 1/2 pick-up loads)
- The house was on a septic but a main sewer line had recently been installed along the front of the house. It had not yet been connected.

Ron and Donna signed an earnest money offer: $200 earnest money, all cash to the seller, with the total purchase price of $2,700.00, and as is condition including all contents in and on the premises. The offer was accepted ten days later by the owner who lived in San Francisco. A $350.00 sales commission was paid to the real estate broker.

All right, that's a pretty good deal, low-priced...but prices were lower back then. So where is the so-called *"miracle?"* Hoped you'd ask!

One or two of the following would scarcely a miracle make. But look at the rest of the true account...the big picture...well, you be the judge:

(1) The one pair of shoes in the closet fit Ron perfectly. They were so comfortable that he wore them often.

(2) When shortened and cleaned the full length fur coat fit Ron's daughter, Beverly, and looked so nice that

she wore it often.

(3) The stole was not mink, but looked beautiful and Ron's wife, Donna, wore it occasionally.

(4) Within a week after the house purchase Ron sold $490.00 worth of antique furniture for cash.

(5) Two of the more valuable pieces of antique furniture, a dresser with mirror and a chest of drawers, were moved to an apartment over Ron's office where they remain to this day, adding to rental value.

(6) The fireplace wood fit perfectly into Ron's new wood stove.

(7) The home was rented for forty months at rents ranging from $95 to $185 per month after which it was sold for nearly five times the original purchase price.

(8) The new owner added a bedroom and double carport, moved in and was still living in the home 15 years later, a highly respected member of the Milton City Council.

(9) Buyer and seller had not seen each other once during those 15 years, but they met at a memorial service for a mutual friend... just two days before this chapter went to the typewriter!

Would this kind of deal interest you, dear reader? If you were to get a call from a Realtor® who had not spoken to you for seven months, offering the property described above for $2,700 cash, would you risk it? And would you call it a miracle? I rest my case.

Incidentally, it was not important to DeBock that his Milton deal fit the theological definition *of "miracle."* The former chaplain knew he was mixing faith and works, sowing seed for a harvest, and witnessing the hand of God through it all. And Ron said, *"Take your seed and start to sow; plan and pray and watch it grow!* Anyone who will do that can expect a similar miracle."

13

The St. Helens Miracle

*"Beauty for ashes; joy instead of mourning; praise
instead of heaviness...You shall be called ministers of our God...You
shall have a double portion of prosperity and everlasting joy."*
- Isaiah 61:3-7

"My, what a smoke she belched!" wrote Junnosuke Izumisawa in a postal card to Ron DeBock, a few days after the explosive eruption of Mt. St. Helens on May 18, 1980. While visiting his Japanese friend in October of the same year, Ron presented him with a vial of volcano ash as a *miyagemono* (souvenir).

"Now this will look nice on your shelf, but take care not to get it mixed up with your ancestors," Ron said, smiling as he handed him the ashes.

About 68 miles north of the famous volcano, ashes provided the ingredient for a miraculous turnaround in a small realty investment made by DeBock in 1970. Ron owned *The St. Helens Apartments*, an old two-story building in downtown Puyallup, one-half block from City Hall.

131

Instinctively, perhaps, DeBock had a nose for what he thought of as "a mustard seed deal" — that is, the kind where he could leverage a tiny amount of cash. With this small seed he would hopefully observe growth and a bumper crop at harvest (proceeds from sale) time.

During the decade of the sixties, Ron's realty investment was limited to single family rental houses. But he looked forward to the day when a low-priced apartment building would come on the market. This might be it!?

St. Helens had all of the earmarks of a solid investment and, hopefully, was good enough to become a mustard seed deal.

The only cash in was $1,444.18 in August, 1970. Ten years later, Ron received $15,000, the down payment on the sale of St. Helens Apartments...in *the same year that Mt. St. Helens spewed forth!*

As it turned out Ron got a mountain of cash out of a mole hill investment. Before hearing the finer points of this amazing story, some facts and figures alone may be of interest:

Purchase of St. Helens Apartments
Date: August, 1970
Price: $29,000
Down Payment: $13,690 including a real estate contract worth $11,590 and oval coffee table valued at $655.82

Sale of St. Helens Apartments
Date: January, 1980
Price: $115,000
Down Payment: $15,000

As you know, prior to the eruption of St. Helens (the mountain) there was a great deal of activity under the surface, for an extended period of time. As early as 1978, volcanic deposits in the vicinity of Mt. St. Helens caused scientists from the U. S. Geological Survey to predict that the volcano would probably erupt "within the next 100 years, and perhaps even before the end of this century." Likewise, during the decade between acquisition and sale of St. Helens (the building), it took a lot of under the-surface activity and churning to result in such growth and visible returns. At the risk of "making a mountain out of a mole hill," a few of the activity highlights might prove interesting.

Chaplain DeBock was assigned to the Third Marine Division on Okinawa at the time he offered to buy the old 7-unit St. Helens Apartments...sight unseen! An ad in his hometown newspaper furnished details of the building for sale by owner.

The monthly gross rents for the seven furnished apartments totalled $430.00. (Rents were low in those days!) On the second floor was an old unfinished bath with two small rooms used for storage. This was changed into an 8th apartment. The cost for remodelling was minimal. Now there were eight apartments, each with three rooms and separate baths.

Fire struck the St. Helens Apartments. It spelled ruin for three of the units and nearly ruined the whole investment. The fire marshal said a tenant's cigarette lodged between a cushion and armrest in an overstuffed chair, where it smoldered for a long time before igniting the vacant unit. No one was injured. The Fire Department was just a block away. The City Building Inspector dutifully advised DeBock that he could not rebuild the existing structure due to county regulations. The insurance coverage was not a problem as those funds were readily available. Ron went to prayer.

About two weeks later the city's building inspector died suddenly. For reasons unknown to DeBock, his successor granted approval to rebuild. Ron did, and the entire building was better than ever. By May, 1980, the month St. Helens (the mountain) blew its top, St. Helens (the building) had a scheduled monthly rental income of $1,530.00. (This was effectively nearly four times the gross rents of a decade earlier, since in 1970 the electricity was included in the rent).

DeBock sold the St. Helens Apartments for $115,000 and received a down payment of $15,000. The $100,000 balance was to be paid interest only for three years (10.5% interest rate) and $1,000 per month beginning the first day of the fourth year after closing.

The arrangement was great. Ron was on top of the mountain, so to speak. He was getting $875 per month from the real estate contract and nothing for three years would come off the principal. Maybe it was worth going through the fire after all, he thought. But if it's St. Helens, don't trust it! How can anyone be sure?

DeBock received the first $1,000 payment in February, 1983. After that…nothing. March went by, April and still nothing! By now two new owners entered the picture. In March, Ron's attorney served a Notice of Declaration of Forfeiture and Cancellation of Contract on all parties who had an interest in the property, giving them a deadline of May 15th by which the entire sum of the real estate delinquencies must be paid in full.

That day, too, came and went. Ron was busily engaged in his local management firm and the days were so full he gradually forgot about St. Helens. A young banker friend invited Ron to lunch in Seattle one Friday in early June. He rushed off telling Donna only that he would be having lunch with Tad up in the big black box which she knew to be the Seafirst Bank building because it looked like the box that the Smith Tower came in.

Lunch was pleasant and Tad mentioned that with interest rates as high as they were, the bank had some excellent CDs available. Since DeBock at the time had very little cash, he was forced to be non-committed.

After lunch the two returned to Tad's office. Tad looked at a message by his phone. "Looks like your wife wants you to call, Ron. You may use my phone." (How did Donna know how to reach that office? She didn't even know Tad's last name! She told the operator that his name was "Tadpole.")

"Of all the days for you to be gone," she began. "There's a check here with your name on it…and, guess for how much?"

"I have no idea. Where is it from?" Ron asked.

"Well, it's from a mortgage and escrow company. **It is for $105,750!**"

"Wow, I'll be right home," Ron said. Before leaving the

office, Ron turned to Tad and said, "Thanks for the chat and fine lunch. And I think I will take you up on a CD next week. I may need a place for about sixty grand."

Owners had to pay off the mortgage to build a new office building at 330 3rd Street S. W. The City of Puyallup later bought the building, naming it the City of Puyallup Development Center.

St. Helens, the mountain, and St. Helens, the building, had something in common. "My, what a smoke she belched!"

14

The Miracle At Key Center

*"And Elisha said unto her, "What shall I do
for thee?...tell me, what hast thou in the house?"
And He asked them, "How any loaves have ye?"*
- 2 Kings 4:2; Mark 8:5

The first word Gary ever spoke was "key." That's because his mother and father both made a big fuss every time
they passed though *Key Center* on the way to Lakebay and
Longbranch.

Gary was 10 $1/_2$ months old when his father, Reverend
Ron DeBock, accepted the pastorate of the two community
churches, Lakebay and Longbranch on the lower Olympic
Peninsula. The churches were only four miles apart, but the
only way to drive to them was via Key Center near Purdy.

The alert, wide-eyed lad soon knew well ahead of arrival
that Key Center was just around the corner. The winding road
provided all of the clues he needed. " K e e y y ! K e e y y ! "
Gary would shout. Mom and dad assured the toddler that he
was right, that Key Center was just ahead.

137

Reverend DeBock served the two churches for 3 $1/_2$ years in the mid-fifties, resigning only when the timing seemed right for taking additional theological studies at Western Evangelical Seminary in Portland, Oregon.

Many years later, long after DeBock concluded his military chaplaincy and had begun a second career in the realty field, he had occasion to put a "FOR SALE" sign on a lot on Palmer Lake, south of Key Center. He carried with him the file with pertinent listing papers, but lacked an up-to-date map of the lots surrounding the lake.

It was a Sunday and Donna agreed to go with her husband on the long trip from Puyallup. In Key Center a modern realty office was open. The salesperson on duty was most helpful. Ron got a map and headed for the lake property. But he left behind the all-important filefolder which he had placed on a desk while looking at the plot map. However, Ron did not know he had left without the file until he had already posted signs at Palmer Lake.

"Where's my file?" Ron asked Donna when he discovered it was missing.

"You had it with you when you went into that office," Donna replied.

"We'll go back. Maybe they're still open. I simply must have that file!" Ron insisted. Indeed the file was critical to Monday's work, and the two-hour round trip from Puyallup (again) would mean cancelling morning appointments. "I sure hope they're open!" Ron said on the way back to Key Center.

But the office was closed...dark...no one in sight. It was also getting dark outside. Ron stood by the front door of the office...just thinking...wondering...thinking some more. There was simply no two ways about it! He spoke out loud, "I absolutely must have that file!" Ron peered into the office window and *saw the folder on a desk*. He looked at the key hole while reaching for a key ring in his pocket. Holding the key ring up to the light he whispered again, "I absolutely must have that file!"

Then Ron remembered the two stories in the Bible which contained such a *"What-can-we-do-now?"* dilemma/predicament. One was the Old Testament story where Elisha asked a poor woman what she had in her house. She replied that she had nothing *except a pot of oil*. As it turned out, God could use *what she did have* — namely, pots...jars...vessels, to hold the miraculous flow of oil. <u>This might be called a special providence miracle.</u>

The other story was that of the 4,000 hungry people without food and about to return to their distant homes. Jesus wanted to know exactly how many loaves were on hand. A few loaves and a few small fish were on hand, but that was hardly enough to feed the thousands of people. Nevertheless, little can be much when God is in it! And here again, God could use *what they had* — loaves and fishes this time — to be the seed for a miracle of multiplication. <u>This was another miracle of special providence.</u>

Surely that is the key for a miracle, Ron thought. He counted the keys on his ring. There were ten. Looking at the door knob, he selected the smallest key on the ring, slipped it effortlessly into the lock, turned the knob, opened the door and picked up his file.

Breathing more deeply, Ron left the office and shut the door behind him. He didn't look back!

Seeing her husband with the file, Donna asked, "How did you get that? Was the door open?"

Smiling big, Ron answered, "I'll tell you later. For now let's just say that they don't call this place *'Key Center'* without a good reason."

15

Stint As
College Professor

"A wise man is
strong; yea, a man of knowledge
increaseth strength."
- Proverbs 24:5

DeBock was invited to join the faculty at Tacoma Community College and to teach in the field of Real Estate beginning the fall term of 1979.

This position would be quite a change of pace for a man of the cloth were it not for the fact that Ron had earned the privilege. Realizing the field of realty investment and residential management would require special knowledge, he enrolled in a two-year degree program at Tacoma Community College.

At the same time, DeBock continued work on a Doctor of Philosophy degree offered by the California Graduate School of Theology in Glendale. He had a Master of Divinity degree and he was only about two years from a doctorate level at that point.

141

Coincidentally, the new Associate degree in real estate and his Ph.D. were both awarded in the spring of 1979. A teaching position was open in the Real Estate course division. They knew Ron and offered him the job.

Upon looking more closely at the class location, Dr. DeBock learned that there was an eager group of real estate students on McNeil Island... yes, prisoners who had time on their hands and, hopefully, wanted to make something out of their lives. It was part of the college's extension class offerings for adult education. Ron decided it would be fun. He signed up.

The class he taught was an introduction to real estate. Between 25 and 30 enrolled. College credit was available to those who qualified.

Class discussion was encouraged. The students were not much different than students in general except for the telltale prisoner garb.

One of the more outspoken prisoners was scheduled to be released the next day following a class he attended in Ron's course. He requested permission to say a few words before the class since this was his final class day. Having received a nod from DeBock, the student left his seat, came to the front and stood in front of the classroom. Dividing his glances between his teacher and the class, he said something like the following:

> *I'd like to thank Dr. DeBock for his fine instruction. I've learned a lot about real estate. I'm leaving tomorrow at last. And do you want to know where I will go? Well...do you remember when Dr. DeBock told us about that rent slot where the renters go to drop their rent in at night or when the rental office is closed? When I get outa here, I'm gonna find that slot. It's my first stop!*

Everybody cracked up, of course. Ron really enjoyed the humor!

Teachers made the trip to McNeil Island by boat. Although it was a short ride from the Steilacoom landing, the Puget Sound waters got choppy when the winds whipped up. For the former tin can chaplain, the bumpy rides revived memories of sea duty. And it was fun again!

At the beginning of the course in real estate, Professor DeBock passed out cards on which he asked the enrolled students to state why they wanted to study real estate. Most of the reasons given fell into the category of a desire to learn about buying and selling or to get a license to work in real estate.

But a few were more revealing. Remember, these were prisoners at McNeil Island:
- *"There's a lot of money in it!"*
- *"cursory perusal of subject to determine whether I wish to pursue it further upon release from incarceration."*
- *"Interested in pursuing investment and development"*
- *"for personal investment purposes"*
- *"I want to have a cool and clear understanding of Real Estate law."*
- *"I'm a carpenter on the streets. Would help later."*

As business sharply increased at DeBock's realty firm, he felt his time would be better spent minding his own business rather than in teaching. But the class on McNeil Island was to be an unforgettable experience, from the boat rides to the slamming doors.

16

Discovering
Land Contracts

*Let's find
a way to supplement
Social Security!*

One of the most exciting discoveries Ron DeBock made as he endeavored to practice what he used to preach was the value of land contracts, also called "real estate contracts." They can be a strong supplement to Social Security benefits.

In a sense, this chapter brings heaven and earth together. The first part (heaven) was prepared for a Sunday School class of senior adults while the second part (earth) was prepared for a real estate class. As will be seen, two of the three unexpected sources for Ron's *faith promise* needs came from pay offs on real estate contracts. What are they? How does one acquire them? That's the story of this chapter. Told by Ron, himself:

My first introduction to a "Faith Promise" came when David Cawston, then pastor at Puyallup First Assembly where

I attended, said that it was money from an unexpected source which you simply have faith that God will provide.

"How could I lose?" I thought. This would be in addition to tithes anyway, so I picked a nice round number: $1,000.00.

My other thoughts were that this promise looked ahead into a full year. So I might expect that the money would come in, perhaps, several months down the road. I made a simple prayer. I only asked God that He would make it crystal clear to me that the money when it came in was that which was to be earmarked for my faith promise. I handed in my faith promise on a Sunday.

The following Tuesday a couple came to my office to make a routine payment of $139.00 on a real estate contract. They had been paying on the contract for years. "We want to know how much we owe you?" Estella Nunnemaker asked with a broader grin than usual.

"$139.00, isn't it," I replied.

"No, what is the balance we owe on the contract?" she countered. I leaned back deeper into my chair.

"Do you mean you want to pay off the entire balance?" I asked, just to be sure I understood.

"Yes, that's right," Bob Nunnemaker chimed in. They gave me a check for $14,552.27. And God said to me, "Is this what you look for?" My *faith promise* had been met in just two days! *On a Tuesday.*

I doubled my faith promise the next year. I thought, "Wow, last year was such adventure...could it happen again like that? Certainly the way to go! Nothing to lose. I am trusting God to being in the money and to show me again clearly that it is coming from such an unexpected source that it cannot be considered regular, earned income." I handed in my faith promise on Sunday.

The following Tuesday I received a call from a mortgage company in Tacoma. "Would you like us to mail this check to you or would you prefer to pick it up?" the lady caller asked.

"What check?" I asked.

"Oh, I thought you knew...sorry, there's a check here for you from the payoff on the Montgomery contract." I picked up the check for $4,900.00 the same day. A church in Tacoma had borrowed funds to consolidate debts among which was this contract owed to me for land sold to the church for additional parking about two years earlier. My *faith promise* had been met in just two days! *On a Tuesday.*

A lot of learning was going on those days! I was learning about real estate contracts. More than that, I was learning lessons of faith. God was my teacher. Faith promises really work! Furthermore, this *Tuesday thing* two years in a row is puzzling. This must be merely a coincidence, I recall thinking...or was it??

It seemed like a long time for that next year to go by. I could hardly wait for October when my pastor would again ask for faith promises! It will not surprise you to hear that I was eager to write out my faith promise. The year had been a good one as two of my businesses had shown substantial successes. Donna made her pledge first. (We do not wish to look at each other's pledges. We feel our giving is that personal!) I made my faith promise on Sunday.

My thoughts while shaving Tuesday morning were that this is the day which the Lord hath made and the logical thing for me to do was to rejoice and be glad in it! (Given the results of the two previous years, do you suppose I had faith for this special day?)

Calls began coming in early Tuesday from a local escrow company and buyers for some lots in Graham which I had purchased seven years earlier. When the fog lifted on the communications of the day, it became clear that the final sale on 9.4 acres fronting on Meridian East at 194th Street would show a profit of more than $200,000.00. For the third year consecutively, my faith promise had been met in just two days! And each time *on a Tuesday.*

Any farmer will tell you that harvesttime depends on conditions outside the control of the sower, factors beyond human management expertise. And farmers also know that your chances of harvesting anything at all is just about nil if you planted no seed.

The biblical promise of earthly "seedtime and harvest"

helped Ron to meet his *faith promise* in the local church. Then he recalled that the pastor asked for those pledges only once a year. But Tuesday comes every week. Think that over!

Land Contracts' Ten-fold Advantages

My own introduction to these fantastic receivables came somewhat as the end-result of a search to delete several smaller rental houses from my inventory in a manner which would "lock-in" an optimum return on my prior investment. In other words, an installment sale might give me twice the gain if I were willing to wait for the money! Moreover, the interest on the loan balance was always much better than I could get on a like amount of cash in a savings account at the time.

In my opinion, real estate contracts can be an ideal supplement to that Social Security stipend during retirement years. Suppose the trusted Social Security system collapsed on your 62nd birthday, you'd still be financially, if not socially, secure. Obviously, the sooner you get started collecting contracts, the better off you will be in retirement.

The following ten advantages which I see in holding real estate contracts is by no means an exhaustive list. But the rubrics will show why I am thoroughly sold on them as a worthwhile addition to any personal investment package:

(1) They make excellent COLLATERAL. If you need cash, your banker will accept your contract(s) as security. (Your loan may even enjoy a lower rate of interest than when borrowing on your signature only. Bankers love contracts!)

(2) They are REDEEMABLE for cash. Although contract purchasers usually make their offers subject to substantial discount rates, you can still get your cash out within a few days. Seasoned contracts (held for at least two years) bearing high interest and having a shorter rate of payoff will not be discounted so much.

(3) They are PYRAMIDABLE. You may wish to use your contract as a down payment on an apartment house or duplex. Depending upon his reasons for selling, the seller may be willing to accept your con-

tract at face value as a portion of the down payment. This means that you can get credit for a comparatively large sum of money which you never had in hand!

(4) They are like an ANNUITY. The money arrives faithfully each and every month just in time to pay your bills (which also arrive each and every month). The proceeds from these contracts afford tremendous returns over a period of years.

(5) They are SAFE. Consider the fact that no one can steal the proceeds due you from a real estate contract. Why? Simply because it represents the source of future income. (If you had sold that house for cash, a thief could relieve you of the sum in a hurry!)

(6) They are SECURE. Secured by the property you have sold, the contract is enforceable. The new owner will usually improve upon the house he has bought. Any improvements will lend security to your contract.

(7) They provide a certain kind of CLOUT. Even a single contract listed on your financial statement affords balance and diversification to your investment portfolio. Accordingly, it enhances your overall borrowing power (much needed if you "wheel and deal" in real estate!)

(8) They have a built-in WINDFALL POTENTIAL.. Occasionally, the holder of a contract will get his property back through default. Since the seller on a contract is still in title until the final payment has been made by the buyer, foreclosure is a relatively simple procedure in a few months. Legal advice is essential. What a bonanza this can be! I sold a house for which the buyer paid $95 per month for about four years. Then the buyer gave a Quit Claim Deed because neither husband nor wife wished to keep the house when they parted company. The buyer's payments exceeded $5,100. Four years later, I sold the house again for 36% more than the original sale price (and for 250% of the original purchase price).

(9) They offer a distinct TAX ADVANTAGE. If your sale qualifies as an installment sale under IRS rules, the capital gain deduction was increased to 60% of your net capital gains from sales made after October, 1978. (Such IRS rules affecting capital gains seem to change frequently, so be careful!) Your contract thus represents a wise alternative to selling for cash. The latter may trigger a traumatic tax event which you may not be prepared to face in the light of other income received that year.

(10) They offer a HIGHER DOLLAR RETURN on your investment. If you can accept a low to moderate down payment, the balance receivable on the contract at current interest rates will inevitably result in larger long-term benefits. For the impatient investor who must have the cash NOW, there can be no such benefits. The rewards are for the patient! It is not unusual for the principal and interest to add up to two or three times the original balance carried by the seller.

How to Collect Real Estate Contracts

Buy a small, lower-priced, fixer-upper house with a low down payment. (You'll have to look harder than in years past, but they are still there!) Make your improvements and rent it to screened tenants for an extended period of time. I suggest that you consider holding the house four to eight years. Then sell it on a real estate contract to a qualified buyer. You should receive 12% to 25% down if possible.

The down payment you receive will now help purchase your second house. It is better to find rental houses near your personal residence as the maintenance will be your responsibility.

The patient investor will discover that the years will be kind to him or her as he/she will profit from all of the well-known benefits of ownership of single-family homes (such as appreciation and tax deductions).

Suggestions on Record-Keeping

I prefer to arrange for my bank to collect the buyer's

contract payments for a year or two. The photocopy of the record of payments which the bank will furnish you at no extra cost will be proof of the promptness and dependability of your buyer/payor.

Eventually, you may desire to keep the records in your own office or home. A printer can prepare forms for you or you may purchase a contract payment book at most office supply stores.

Avoid the Temptation to Sell

You will be wise in allowing those hard-earned (?) contracts to pay off over their natural life rather than selling at a heavy discount. Of course, the cash is always available if you feel you must sell. In the event that your decision is to sell a real estate contract, shop around for the best rate (lowest discount) available.

A preferred way to get cash benefits from contracts is to use them for security at the bank. As previously mentioned, bankers love them. Your banker may or may not require an actual assignment of the contract, depending on how much you plan to borrow.

Stretch Your Imagination a Moment!

If you could somehow start at the age you will be two years from now and buy one house each year for ten years, renting them until all mortgages were paid off, and selling them on 25-year contracts at current interest rates, what effect might such a plan have upon your retirement income? I hope you will take the time to consider such a plan—or even a bolder one!

Length of the Holding Period

How long should a single family house be held as a rental unit before selling? The answer to this question can make the difference between strong or weak gains in your investment planning. As owner you have many options. Timing of the sale can be crucial and deserves careful thought.

Writers (who are also investors) do not seem to be in

151

agreement on the matter. Some favor relatively rapid turn-over of properties while others advise that you should never sell a home that is considered "a winner." I personally favor retention of the rental until such time as the mortgage is paid off or nearly so. But if a strong buyer happens on the scene at a time when I need investment capital, I may "lock-in" my investment via a contract sale. Hold for eight to ten years, if possible.

Be sure to study the fine-tuning of contract preparation as well as how you may sell a portion (certain number of months) of your contract instead of selling the entire contract. For example, if your buyer is willing to pay off the property in five years, you will not need to wait so long for your money. likewise, if you can sell sixty months of your contract, this may reduce the principal by a relatively small amount, and you still have the biggest part of your contract for future income.

Timing of the sale should be in light of the general business cycle. If it is a "seller's market" the sale price will be higher than in times when the nation is in a recession. (Keep this in mind when buying, too!) Since you will probably discover that "appreciation" was even kinder to you than the cash flow overage you received from rents (the difference between the rent you received and the payments you made on the house), the longer you keep the house as a rental the better the picture on selling.

Ground Rules for Maintenance

When you buy a small rental house, settle on one that is structurally sound and one that has the right things wrong with it. Keep in mind that you must keep it in habitable condition. If you are fortunate enough to buy a house that needs such improvements as painting, landscaping, remodel-led kitchen, new carpets or replacement of a sagging porch, it may be a profitable investment! Or find one that needs exactly what YOU can provide.

Generally, you should receive enough income from rents to hire most of the maintenance. Of course, some investors prefer to perform much of the work themselves. This is especially true of beginning investors and lends safety to the investment in the light of the economic realities of high costs of labor and materials. As your portfolio of houses grows, you may wish to hire a handyman (or several) to perform most or all of the maintenance.

Tips on Good Management

During the holding period before selling your rental house on a real estate contract, the following tips may be helpful:

(1) Know your tenants. Make sure they do not sublet.

(2) Use a legally defensible, iron-clad lease agreement which provides for a late fee if rents are not paid within a 3-day grace period.

(3) Arrange for tenants to pay rents at your office or home. Do not collect rents, with rare exceptions.

(4) Be firm about the due dates for rents.

(5) Be flexible when it comes to improvements—especially if a capable tenant will perform work as you provide materials.

(6) Do not increase rents without a letter furnishing justification for doing so, substantiated by facts (increase in property taxes, etc.). Give forty-five or more days notice. November is a good month for rent to be increased.

(7) Arrange for the tenant(s) to pay all utilities if possible.

(8) Accept cash only for the first month's rent and deposit.

(9) Always get a security deposit to cover excess cleaning or damage. Such deposit should be equivalent to a month's rent if possible.

(10) Get the first and last month's rent if possible.

(11) Review the landlord/tenant rules applicable to your area and keep a copy of such rules handy for reference.

(12) Screen your applicants carefully. A tenant problem can usually be blamed on inadequate screening which

should include a credit check, an employment check and previous landlord(s) check.

17

The Mt. Sinai Miracle

"And when forty years were expired,
there appeared to him in the wilderness of Mount Sinai
an angel of the Lord in a flame of fire in a bush."
- Acts 7:30

This amazing true story cannot be fully appreciated unless the reader understands two basic ecclesiastical and biblical truths:

(1) The Baptism in the Holy Ghost is for all Christian believers, and according to The Statement of Fundamental Truths of the General Council of the Assemblies of God, "is witnessed by the initial physical sign of speaking with other tongues as the Spirit of God gives them utterance."

Many churches consider the *Pentecostal experience* to be one of the cardinal truths of the Bible, a phenomenon of the early Christian believers and available for all believers down to the present time. For example, the International Church of the Foursquare Gospel holds the Baptism in the Holy Ghost is one of its four main doctrines, alongside of salvation, divine healing and the second coming of Christ. Article V of the Statement of Fundamental Truths of the General Council of the Assemblies of God, paragraphs 7 and 8 state:

7. The Baptism in the Holy Ghost

All believers are entitled to and should ardently expect and earnestly seek the promise of the Father, the baptism in the Holy Ghost and fire, according to the command of our Lord Jesus Christ. This was the normal experience of all in the early Christian church. With it comes the enduement of power for life and service, the bestowment of the gifts and their uses in the work of the ministry (Luke 24:49; Acts 1:4,8; I Corinthians 12:1-31). This experience is distinct from and subsequent to the experience of the new birth (Acts 8:12-17; 10:44-46; 11:14-16; 15:7-9). With the baptism in the Holy Ghost come such experiences as an overflowing fullness of the Spirit (John 7:37-39; Acts 4:8), a deepened reverence for God (Acts 2:43; Hebrews 12:28), an intensified consecration to God and dedication to His work (Acts 2:42), and a more active love for Christ, for His Word, and for the lost (Mark 16:20).

8. The Initial Physical Evidence of the Baptism in the Holy Ghost

The baptism of believers in the Holy Ghost is witnessed by the initial physical sign of speaking with other tongues as the Spirit of God gives them utterance (Acts 2:4). The speaking in tongues in this instance is the same in essence as the gift of tongues (I Corinthians 12:4-10,28), but different in purpose and use.

(2) *Forty years* must be a favorite time frame for our Father in heaven. That period of time appears in the Bible again and again. The most familiar of these is probably the forty years during which the children of Israel wandered in the wilderness near Mt. Sinai:

"Do you remember how the Lord led you through the wilderness for all those forty years, humbling you and testing you to find out how you would respond, and whether or not you would really obey him? Yes, he humbled you by letting you go hungry and then feeding you with manna, a food previously unknown to both you and your ances-

156

*tors. He did it to help you realize that food comes by obeying every command of God. **For all these forty years** your clothes haven't grown old, and your feet haven't been blistered or swollen."*

- *Deuteronomy 8:2-4*

But that's just the beginning! Kings reigned *for forty years.* Isaac was *forty years old* when he married Rebekah. Esau married Judith *at the age of forty.* The conquest of Midian was so decisive during the lifetime of Gideon that "Midian never recovered, and the land was at peace *for forty years."* (Ju. 8:28) And on and on it goes! It is significant that the Bible contains no less than 38 *40-year periods of time!*

Now forty years is a long time in anyone's life! It's the lion's share of the biblical "three score and ten." (Ps. 90:10)

As a teenager, Ron DeBock was an ardent Bible student. And in the flyleaf of his Bible were written two dates: November 27, 1944, the day he accepted Jesus Christ as his personal Savior and *March 13, 1945,* the day he was baptized in the Holy Ghost. The latter experience occurred in Shelton, Washington, at the Church of the Foursquare Gospel.

Upon graduating from Northwest College and entering pastoral ministry nearly a decade later, DeBock bought a big deluxe Pastoral Record book into which he transferred important historic dates. Among them, of course, was March 13, 1945, that memorable day when he received the gift of the Holy Ghost.

Decades later after a career of civilian and military assignments in the ministry, Ron DeBock had a chance to take a trip to the Holy Land. It was a group tour sponsored by his alma mater, Northwest College in Kirkland. A chance of a lifetime for a minister, the tour was known as the Northwest College Flying Seminar and was led by Dr. Amos Millard, well-known guide and authority on the holy land.

Dates for the 1985 Flying Seminar were March 3 - 17. Ron was one of twenty-seven on the Holy Land tour.

DeBock thought the entire tour was exciting. Every day was filled with awesome experiences. All stops were well-planned by Dr. Millard, the Flying Seminar Coordinator.

It was such a busy itinerary that Ron paid little attention to the planned sight-seeing stops until a day or two before the group would visit.

Ron pulled out his printed itinerary just before bedtime in Eilat, a beautiful resort city on the Red Sea, where they stayed overnight. He noted that they were at the foot of Mt. Sinai and that the next day they would, if they felt they could do so, climb to the top of this rugged peak where God revealed Himself in awesome holiness to Moses and gave the nation of Israel the Law.

Ron wanted to climb Mt. Sinai. *But it had not entered his mind that to do so would put him on the mountain exactly forty years (to the day!) from the day he had the Pentecostal experience according to Acts 2:4 and was baptized in the Holy Ghost.*

Very early in the morning, Ron was awake while still in bed...just thinking about the adventure ahead of him...to climb Mt. Sinai. Then he somehow thought about dates. He thought of how God had led him through a lifetime of ministry and abundance. How many years had he been living for Jesus Christ? What would his life have been without God in it? And how long has it been since he accepted Christ as Savior? All of these and other thoughts raced through his brain!

Then suddenly...he began calculating actual dates...lo, and behold, it will be *40 years to the day* since I knelt in the prayer room of that little Foursquare Church in Shelton and was filled with the Holy Spirit!

There you have it! The next day found an ordained minister of the Assemblies of God kneeling on the top of Mt. Sinai. His prayer was filled with gratitude for it all. And from that pinnacle Ron could see the same wilderness where the Israelites spent...how long?...*forty years!*

18

Rotary Club
Of Puyallup

*"Real Happiness is
Helping Others"*

When Puyallup Rotarians Paul Hackett and Art Larson sat down in Ron's office in the spring of 1990 to invite DeBock to join their club, the timing could not have been better. The year was already off to a good start with real estate values up and sales of long-term investments doing well.

Their pitch was low-key. (Rotary sells itself). Ron had worked with Paul on a few local sales and knew him to be a distinguished graduate of Princeton Theological Seminary, a former Presbyterian minister and pastor. Like Ron, Mr. Hackett made a transition from ministry into real estate.

Paul introduced Art Larson, a former high school principal and a man with perfect attendance in the Rotary Club of Puyallup for 19 years. These two men explained Rotary International's four reasons for existence:

159

Object of Rotary

The object of Rotary is to encourage and foster the ideal of service as a basis of worthy enterprise and, in particular, to encourage and foster:

(1)   The development of acquaintance as an opportunity for service;

(2)   High ethical standards in business and professions; the recognition of the worthiness of all useful occupations; and the dignifying by each Rotarian of his occupation as an opportunity to serve society;

(3)   The application of the ideal of service by every Rotarian to his personal, business and community life;

(4)   The advancement of international understanding, good will, and peace through a world fellowship of business and professional men united in the ideal of service.

Ron was impressed with the objectives of Rotary International. Here was a service club with world-wide acceptance offering opportunities for service above self and fellowship with local business and professional people. It was almost biblical in its standards. Ron especially liked the:

FOUR - WAY TEST
(1) Is it the Truth?
(2) Is it fair to all concerned?
(3) Will it build good will and better friendships?
(4) Will it be beneficial to all concerned?

"May I look over this packet of information about the club and call you?" Ron asked.

"Fine, here's my card. You can reach me best at my office," Paul replied.

Ron looked over the material and checked the encyclopedia concerning the well-known service club. Of course, he already knew about Rotary in a general way, but he wanted to study its history. He learned that Rotary was founded in 1905 by a Chicago attorney, Paul P. Harris, to promote the ideal of *service to others* and to encourage high ethical standards in business and the professions.

The local Rotary Club of Puyallup had more than seventy members at the time, five of whom had more than ten years' perfect attendance. The local club awarded monetary awards and scholarships to selected students in junior and senior high schools in Puyallup. An exchange study program was also sponsored.

Internationally, the club had more than 1 million members belonging to over 20,000 Rotary clubs in more than 150 countries. Rotary shows a love and compassion for the disabled, the hungry and the underprivileged, many of whom are the beneficiaries of approximately 25,000 service projects performed by Rotary Clubs around the world each year. The *Youth Exchange* program alone sends over 6,000 young people of high school age abroad for a school year or a holiday.

It was not long before Ron called Paul Hackett. "I'm sold on Rotary! I'm ready to join. If you'd have asked me last year, I would have said I was simply too busy with the business. But, now I think I need a club like Rotary. When can we get together?" That was it. Paul Hackett came back to Ron's office for the check required for "Sustaining Member," assuring him that it was a wise decision, because Rotary is a lot of fun.

The local club was not only lots of fun for Ron, but afforded just the kind of business acquaintanceships which he lacked and needed. He did have the fellowship of church members, but Rotary offered wide contacts in the business and professional fields of vocation. A program chairman for the month would usually arrange for an interesting speaker or activity at the Wednesday noon luncheon meeting held at the Puyallup Elks facility.

Puyallup was dear to Ron's heart. He would not have seriously considered joining a Rotary Club in any other town.

What's so special about Puyallup?

Ron was not born in Puyallup. He was born in Buckley, but as soon as he could walk, he left town. At least that's what he likes to tell people. (Buckley is a small town about twenty miles east of Puyallup).

Puyallup is a quaint village-like community of slightly more than 25,000 people. The housing is a mix including ageless antiques from turn-of-the-century Victorians to modern contemporaries in subdivisions with very restrictive covenants.

One can hop on a bicycle and ride for miles to a nearby town such as Fife, Sumner or Orting without climbing any hills. Head south, though, and you'll be climbing steep hills in a hurry. South is the direction where the population growth is the most noticeable.

The sixth largest fair in the nation is in Puyallup. The Puyallup Fair attracts well over a million visitors annually and provides thousands of jobs. The non-profit corporation has grown bigger and better since it began in the year 1900. Besides, it's lots of fun! If the rides don't capture your fancy, the smell of onions on the "fair burgers" will.

Puyallup may have just about the richest soil in the whole world. "Ya put an ol' cedar fence post in the ground and it'll go ta buddin'!" was the way the late Chuck Bond described the soil's growing quality. Mr. Bond should know. He owned the highly successful Bond's Blueberry Farm in Puyallup. And why wouldn't you believe a man like Chuck? (In college days he played in the Rose Bowl with the University of Washington Huskies!)

While Ron stopped short of endorsing the fence post story, he noted that Joel Holland, a battalion chief for the Puyallup Fire Department, grew an 827-pound squash in Puyallup soil which set a *world record*. The giant squash earned Holland first place in the World Pumpkin Confederation weigh-in in Vacaville, California, in October, 1992.[165]

A letter Ron wrote to the editor of a local newspaper stirred up a few townsfolk, judging by the numerous comments which followed it's appearance in the Herald. Perhaps, this letter will help illustrate better than anything else Ron's fondness for his little hometown:[166]

High on the Valley

Editor:
I think the toughest experience in my life was saying goodbye to

my wife and three children as I shipped out for combat tours with the Third Marine Division in Vietnam.

Puyallup was the focal point for me. My family was here. Mail from home with Puyallup on the postmark was the mail I read first.

Now, more than 20 years later, I love Puyallup even more than then. It has been a growing love.

Puyallup gave my first job picking strawberries at age 10. I quickly learned the worth of a dollar! Puyallup gave me a wife (we met at Puyallup High School) and educated my children.

And how I love the Fair! Ah, there it is! **Do the Puyallup!** *Who needs drugs? Not me! There are other highs in this valley.*

Look closely at the name "Puyallup." I have heard that it means "generous people." But look closer. There are three syllables. (A trinity is akin to something divine!) The accent is on the center or heart of the name which tells me how many people in the world have sinned. **All,** *as well as how many things work together for good to them that love God (Romans 8:28).*

The first syllable, to me, is not **Puy** *(no tideflats here), but is Pew since the seat of worship has been and remains the most meaningful activity for this veteran. To "be filled with the Spirit" (Eph. 5:18) is to experience a high that no drugs can equal.*

The third syllable tells me the direction which the saints of God will go when the rapture of the church takes place, according to one of St. Paul's epistles to the Thessalonians. And I might add that the last syllable of our city's name points direction to any person who wants to stop abusing himself with drugs: **give UP!**

While the Puyallup valley gave Ron an unmistakable feeling of "home," he can thank South Hill for giving him his wife. Donna lived there. A courtship of five years, including absences, ended in matrimony in 1949.

Lake Surprise was on North Hill, west of Meridian. Ron frequently swam there where the high dives were fun. Platforms were at levels of ten feet, twenty feet, thirty, on up to fifty feet!

Returning home from the lake on his bike one day, Ron's bicycle chain fell off...down the steep North Meridian hill! A 10-year-old boy barely negotiated the final turn at breakneck speed. No hand brakes. Only the foot brake...and no chain! Nonetheless, due to the grace of God, Ron would live to enjoy Al Hibbler's best-selling vocal record, *"Unchained Melody,"* which wouldn't appear until seventeen years later. Much later yet, appeared the popular exclamation, *"Give me a break!"* Or was that spelled B-R-A-K-E?

At a noon meeting in September 1992, the Puyallup Fair was in full swing and the Rotary Club of Puyallup still had twelve busy days to keep their fund-raising concession open day and night. The booth was an important annual project. Also, on the day prior to the club meeting, primary elections were held statewide. Ron's invocation picked up on both events:

Some will attain a high office;
Others will be put on the shelf
Meanwhile, here at Rotary (things haven't changed)
It's still "Service Above Self!"

We've found one sure way to help our youth
And demonstrate that we CARE:
It's when, Dear Lord, we can man the booth
At the Western Washington Fair.

So with others who SERVE, we'll get up our nerve
And ask for God's help with this prayer:
"Help us do as we ought and give our best shot
By manning the booth at the Fair!"
Amen.

For theology students, D.D.s, pastors, and other clerics, it might be important to know that Ron used a lead-in of "Our gracious Father in heaven, we come to you now in Christ's Name."

Past Presidents of the Puyallup Rotary Club were men of renown whose names make an impressive list of civic leaders who served the club since its formation in 1948. The late Glen Walsworth was one of those on the list.

Glen Walsworth was President of the Puyallup Rotary Club in 1962-63. While Ron DeBock knew that Glen was a very active Rotarian, he first heard that Glen had 34 years' perfect attendance from remarks at the memorial service following his death in December of 1990. Glen was Donna's brother and, therefore, Ron's brother-in-law. At the time of his death, Glen had been employed by Washington Natural Gas for 34 years, having worked his way up to be district manager. Smart and dependable, Glen was a devout church-goer and did a lot of "practicing" what his pastor preached.

When the local Rotary club discovered that Ron was a man of the cloth, he was asked to give the invocation at luncheon meetings. (These brief prayers are a customary part of the order of each Rotary meeting). A few of his invocations had endings that rhymed:

> Mere words that are nice will hardly suffice;
> As we pray we must roll up our sleeves.
> If we hold back our gift we have not paid the price,
> (For who gives is the one who receives.)

> We stand in prayer in our city fair
> With Rotary's sisters and brothers.
> May the food be blessed for members and guests,
> And our aim be SERVICE TO OTHERS.

Ron's prayers would sometimes recognize the topic of the speaker on the day's program, for the fun enjoyed by the club levying "fines" (as an interesting means of raising funds), or for working at a fair booth:

> To many of us who have lived here so long,
> This Valley just cannot be beat.
> We thank Thee, dear Lord, we could never be bored
> With this moist air and not humid heat!
> For life, for food, for peace and HEALTH,
> For Rotary's boost to our living,
> (Such benefits extend beyond mere wealth),

O Lord, You never stop GIVING!

Our speaker's message must be heard;
Let our YOUTH be all they can be,
They should claim the promise in Your Word:
"The TRUTH shall make you free."

Now God, we give thanks for fun and for PRANKS,
Even FINES that do sometimes embarrass.
As a club we just know You want us to grow,
As foreseen by the late great Paul Harris.

With others who SERVE, we might get up our nerve
And ask for God's help with this prayer:
"Help me do as I ought and give my best shot
By manning the booth at the Fair."

Now let enthusiasm at each table
Show we're glad to be back again.
Help us to SHARE as we are able!
In Jesus' Name, Amen.

There is one essential basic truth:
We must demonstrate that we CARE:
Perhaps, dear Lord, we can man the BOOTH
At the Western Washington Fair.

Speaking of prayers, the Puyallup Rotary Club just happens to have an excellent representation of local clergymen in the membership. Accordingly, invocations given by these professional men were occasionally, as you will appreciate, put together in words beyond the amateur level. (Please do not misunderstand. To be sure, God hears us all...and knows all hearts!) One of the most notable of these men, the Reverend Dr. Erv Gerken, member of the Puyallup club since 1959 and Past-President in 1964-65, was especially eloquent. His invocations were at all times fitting and proper—appropriate. So, when Ron asked President-Elect Don Johnson to give the invocation the next week after Erv's prayer, Don's immediate response was, "Hey, why pick me? When those Lutherans pray, they can pray around the world...but, with me, it's just Rubba dub dub ...thanks for the grub!" Such humility!

There's bound to be some serendipitous discoveries for members of a local service club. One of these began when club member Bob Snyder invited Ron and Donna to his home to hear about a ministry in Turlock, California.

To Ron's surprise, Bob's son, Scott, had started an outreach near California State University under the auspices of *Chi Alpha College Ministries*, an Assemblies of God endeavor for youth. Ron was impressed with Scott and Kristen Snyder and their ministry which they shared with a slide presentation and question-answer session before members of the local Bethany Baptist Church and other friends. One of the satisfying elements of the evening was the discovery that denominational labels do mean a lot less than many suppose. Here was a former banker, whom he admired as a devout Baptist believer and, of course, senior active club member. But he never knew that Bob had a son and daughter-in-law engaged in a youth ministry within the Assemblies of God, the denomination which had endorsed Ron as a Navy chaplain and with which he had been ordained since 1953.

Was there any practical lesson to be learned from the foregoing experience shared by two Rotarians? Yes, Ron reflected upon the fact that Paul Harris envisioned the development of relationships which encompassed business and professional people who could unite for service to others. By the same token, the Christ portrayed in the synoptic Gospels of the New Testament encouraged a practical love and caring for others as a demonstration of true brotherhood. Perhaps, this emphasis was the most vivid in His own story known as the Good Samaritan. (Luke 10:30-37)

It can be said without fear of contradiction that service clubs and churches alike would do well to minimize the importance of their differences and seek optimum service to humanity—via a love that genuinely cares. There is no reason in the world why clubs and churches cannot cooperate in the achievement of common goals. Has anyone put forth a conscious effort to get them together? In unity there is strength!

On the local level, the Puyallup Rotary Club has been very active in the support of youth projects such as baseball teams, students of the month at high schools and gift-makers for needy children in the community. On an international level, Rotary International has recently contributed over $200,000,000.00 in the fight against polio. What strength there is in unity!

The officers and directors of Puyallup Rotary Club for 1992-1993 were:

- DON JOHNSON
  President
- LARRY CARNEY
  President Elect
- STAN JACKSON
  Secretary
- MIKE NELSON
  Treasurer
- MARTY WARR
  Club Service
- CHERYL LANGELAND
  Community Service
- HERB BROOKS
  Vocational Service
- DEEN POPOOLA
  International Service
- TIM JACOBS
  Past President

The Rotary International President for 1992-93 was Clifford L. Dochterman of Stockton, California.

The Puyallup Rotary Club Past Presidents were:

*Willam P. Wotton	1948
Bruce D. Robertson	1949
Frank A. Peters	1950
*Charles E. Bond	1951
*George Maloney (Past District Gov.)	1952

*Walter H. Dassel	1953
*Roben O. Logan	1954
*Marion F. Catron	1955
Ronald H. Crowe	1956
*Lawrence R. Berg	1957
Paul K. Parkhurst	1958
*Buryl B. Bryan	1959
Arthur C. Jerstad	1960
Norbert E. Grove	1961
*Glen Walsworth	1962
Sanford T. Shaub	1963
Erwin A. Gerken	1964
*Charles S. Rankin	1965
Robert Evans	1966
*William L. Bowers	1967
*Vincent C. Westover	1968
Archie E. Heany	1969
Daniel R. Cooper	1970
*John M. Engerson	1971
E. Arthur Larson	1972
Terence S. Davies	1973
J. Burton Salter	1974
Ray Tobiason	1975
Lee Ozmun	1976
Larry McVittie	1977
Hollis H . Barnett	1978
Pearce A. Dressel	1979
*Scott Minnich	1980
Lorin Ginther	1981
Richard B. Crowe	1982
John Bustad	1983
Bob Dalton	1984
Chuck Jackson	1985
Norm Gerken	1986
Jay Mensonides	1987
Don Mott	1988
Robert A. Yost	1989
David L. Berntsen	1990

Tim Jacobs   1991
  *Deceased

It should be pointed out that membership is by invitation only. New members are given a red badge with name and classification. After three months' perfect attendance and the completion of several club activities, a permanent blue badge is awarded. Ron wore his red badge for an extended period of time. It took no less than fourteen months! (The hard part for Ron was the requirement of three months' perfect attendance). But, to his surprise, he was made chairman of...you guessed it...the Attendance Committee!

At the beginning of his third year in the club, Ron was chairman of this important committee. Why? Then he found the answer. He was reading the chapter entitled *"Ways to Improve and Stimulate Attendance,"* provided by the Rotary Club Assistant Director of Club Service. One of the ideas which caught Ron's eye was the following:

Members with lowest attendance records are sometimes assigned to the attendance committee— with surprisingly positive results.

There it is, Ron thought...his attendance at the weekly meetings had been poor. He was not proud of the poor record. Conflicts in scheduling came all too often. But, at least now he knew why he was made chairman of the Attendance Committee. If surprising results are sometimes achieved by assigning members with lowest attendance records to the attendance committee, it follows that if he or she has the lowest record of attendance of them all . . . there's our chairman!

What service club doesn't have a problem maintaining high levels of attendance? Competition is often keen among area-wide clubs and club members take pride in achieving enviable attendance levels in the district. As chairman of the attendance committee at the Puyallup Rotary Club for the 1992-93 year, Ron was assigned the task of preparing for the club president some guidelines and procedures which the club should follow to improve club attendance at weekly meetings. It was a routine assignment and not difficult to put together.

Happily, Ron discovered that what they were after fell neatly into an acrostic which may be both useful and a bit of fun, too: A Club Attendance Support Team (CAST) was necessary. So Ron drafted a memo to President Don Johnson which pointed out that:

(1) The attractiveness of any production depends a lot on its CAST of characters.

(2) Whenever we support a single member to improve his or her attendance, we *cast* another vote for a better club.

(3) Rather than being quick to *cast* a member out via strict club attendance rules, we should be ready to lend support to that member who needs our help.

(4) Any member in the club who helps club attendance is considered a member of the Club Attendance Support Team (CAST):

CAST Daffynitions[167]

body cast a member finds that the entire club is willing to go to almost any extreme to get him or her to improve club attendance

castaway a would-be supporter, but he/she is somewhere vacationing and unavailable to help

castigate a cover-up of the real reason for failing to help a member with poor attendance

cast iron a golf club which a team member uses as a weapon on a lackadaisical Rotarian

cast off a support team member who completely misses the mark when dealing with a member whose attendance is falling off

castrate   a graph which illustrates the success rate of support team members

downcast   a dejected attendance support member who just had a real bad experience trying to save the day for a club member whose attendance has hit the skids

fly casting   a member who specializes in helping the jet set and airline pilots to get serious about their make-up meetings in far-away places

outcast   a Rotarian whose attendance level is too low to afford maximum effectiveness in the role of encouraging another member to improve his/her record of attendance

Glen Walsworth
(Donna's brother had 34 years of perfect
attendance in the Rotary Club of Puyallup)

19

Mother Of All
Capital Gains

*"...If you give, you will get! Your gift will return to you in
full and overflowing measure, pressed down, shaken together to make room
for more, and running over. Whatever measure you use to give—
large or small—will be used to measure what is given back..."*
- Luke 6:38, TLB

Everyone has a best year, one that outshines them all.
Ron DeBock had his, too. And it was a beaut!

One thing you must know. Ron kept good records. Charts
on income and expenses, graphs on trends, growth and such.
In the days before computers were so sophisticated, he did it
the old-fashioned way...with a calculator! Comparisons were
made on everything from composite equity gains to amor-
tized net gains on real estate contracts.

Losses would have been recorded, too, if there were any.
Most years were good years for real estate in the sixties and
seventies in the Pacific Northwest. Rents kept creeping up
almost as rapidly as the cost of maintenance. But Ron didn't
always bat a thousand! There was the time when a gentleman
(?) in one of his Tacoma duplexes got mad at his wife and left

home. A couple of hours later he called her.

"I'm very mad and I'll find a way to get even with you!" he said. He returned and set fire to the duplex, burning it for a total loss. Next day's newspaper carried an article entitled: ARSONIST JAILED FOR $8,000 FIRE. All of this would have been bad enough. Due to a technicality, the duplex was not covered by insurance. It was a mistake Ron would not make again! The only thing that saved the day was the tax treatment of the loss. (We do best when we profit by someone else's mistake, but we *absolutely must* profit from our own mistakes.)

Getting back to the banner year...it was 1990. Seattle and the Puget Sound region was enjoying a year of increased sales at higher-than-ever prices. The word was out. Such peaks in the industry do not last long. The market can be so uncertain that by the time you realize it's a seller's market, sales and prices have dropped.

Ron sold three rental properties for cash that year: a home in Marysville, Washington for $90,000, a home in Woodinville, Washington for $103,600 and Park Place Apartments (4 units) in Puyallup, Washington for $103,500. He held the homes for five years each, using rents to reduce the mortgages. The apartments were held for sixteen years.

The appreciation was substantial on each property:

Marysville:
Purchased for $60,074 with $6,739 down
SOLD FOR $ 90,000

Woodinville:
Purchased for $66,444 with $6,739 down
SOLD FOR $103,600

Puyallup:
Purchased for $22,500 with $2,000 down
SOLD FOR $103,500

On the surface, this looks like a good year for capital gains. Yes... and No! Ron's capital gain for 1990 (IRS Form 1040) was $148,925 and total income of $151,497. If he is going to practice what he preached, IRS gets a check for $35,930! And since Ron was determined to *practice what he preached,*

IRS did get $35,930 for 1990. Numbers are all relative? Yes, all for *"Uncle Sam!"*

That was more money than he had earned in all of his years as pastor of civilian churches. Easy come, easy go? No, hard come, harder go!

It can be argued that it is not wise to sell rental property. However, values were up in that year. Moreover, the two houses were distant from Ron's personal residence and office. As for the apartment building, the new owner requested that Ron's management firm, Rainier Rentals, also manage the four units after closing of the transaction. The new owner was the City of Puyallup, which also owned the property across the street known as the City of Puyallup Development Center, situated on land formerly owned by Ron. See Chapter, *The St. Helens Miracle.* Rainier Rentals agreed to continue management of the Park Place Apartments, now managed by the firm without a break since 1974.

A great many factors have a bearing upon the worthwhileness of selling three properties for cash in a single year. The tax bite can be a big bite as has been shown. Some obvious considerations will include the age, health and investment portfolio of the owner. What are his goals and his ambitions? How is the market for sales? How do current capital gains laws affect the sales? Would contract sales, for example, be preferred to cash? The answers to these questions will vary with investors.

A bonanza harvest in a single year can cost you plenty. Once the required tax and other costs are factored in, such cash sales might very well meet the investor's alienation criteria. The point is to have a plan going in and coming out. Holding rental units deserves an investment strategy. In other words, the acquisition of a dozen or more rental houses might become more to handle than previously imagined. And all of the while as homes were purchased, it might never have occurred to the investor that one day he or she will want to sell. There are as many ways to sell as there are to buy a rental property.

Since Ron's involvement in rental units was comparatively heavy, it became increasingly important to decide the volume level he wished to maintain in later years. Doing a *good job* of managing just a few units might be better than having too many to handle properly. And for that matter, doing a poor job of management would hardly be practicing what he preached, would it?

How does a preacher measure financial success?

That's an easy one. You measure it the same way everyone else does. You look at your profit and loss statements and your balance sheets. You look at your net worth, and there you have it. Right? Wrong!

It's not that simple. In a very real sense, a Christian preacher has pecuniary assets which emanate from an experiential understanding of biblical teaching on the subject. Most of them have lived by faith. For many, the prayer "Give us this day our daily bread" became exactly that: a prayer for daily bread!

On the other hand, America has had it up to here (right hand under chin, palm down) with ostentatious televangelists. These miss the wisdom of Solomon by a country mile: "Give me neither poverty nor riches; feed me with food convenient for me: Lest I be full and deny thee, and say, 'Who is the Lord?'"...[168] There is no lack of biblical teaching on the pitfalls of riches.

Incidentally, Ron and Donna became "Lifetime Partner" of Jim Bakker's PTL by sending $2000. A letter dated March 19, 1984, reads in part:

Dear Dr. DeBock,

Congratulations! You are now a Lifetime Partner of the NEW PTL Partner Center here at Heritage USA! I'm so excited that you have chosen to be a part of one of the greatest projects in the history of PTL.

As a Lifetime Partner, you will be able to enjoy some tremendous privileges. First, you will be able to spend up to four days and three nights at the Heritage Grand Hotel free, every year, for the rest of your life.

Five paragraphs followed. The letter, written on hotel stationery, was signed simply "Jim." (The accompanying member card 1377 056 2 is NonTransferable.)

At the time, Ron thought it was a good project and worthy of a $2000 check. Eventually he felt that he was not only duped, but duped by one of the ministers of his own church, the Assemblies of God.

There must be a lesson to be learned from such a fiasco as this. Is it not that the love of money is a root that insists on breaking ground sooner or later? How attractive and inviting the plant appears at first!

A Methodist minister friend reminded Ron of John Wesley's word to those of his societies who, having been converted from lives wasted in drink and folly, now found themselves prospering and even growing rich. The danger was, that being secure in material comforts, they were forgetting the Savior who had delivered them from sin. What shall we do with money, then? Make all you can! Save all you can! Give all you can! Thank you, Mr. Wesley!

Preachers are God's servants. Ron believed this implicitly. There are eternal rewards for His servants which will transcend earthly gains. To see a preacher in it for financial enrichment cheapens the calling.

Nevertheless, these ministers in local churches are deserving of a fine salary and benefits, commensurate with experience and maturity. If the church fails to provide an adequate salary for its preacher(s), a lack of full disclosure of salary levels may be partly to blame. Statistics do reveal that pastors are paid too little, not too much. This level needs to be raised when feasible. They are often worth far more than we give them.

Spending says a lot about wealth.

IRS does not tax wealth, it taxes income. In general, those who are willing to save and put their money into investments, will become wealthy. These compulsive savers and investors soon enter the growing pool of well-heeled Americans.

Annual income has a short life. Spend it all on consumer

goods to the neglect of saving and investing just means you start all over again next year. To save and invest early in life is bound to pay "dividends" later in life. The best wealth accumulators tend to favor investment, not consumption!

Never mind the *amounts* to be set aside for investment. Simply use the *percentages.* Then stick with it! For example, you can budget ten percent of gross income for saving. Do it. Christian believers will be tithing double, first to God and second to self. Watch the gain for both heaven and earth!

Real Estate is still a good investment

Ron was one of those compulsive savers. Then he bought real estate in the form of income rental units. By late 1992, when this book was nearing completion, he had invested in:[169]

> 34 single family homes, 2 duplexes, a tri-plex, an 8-unit apartment, 3 mobile homes on their own lot, 5 lots rented to mobile home owners, an office building with one overhead apartment, a church with 3-bedroom parsonage, and six acreage sites: 5 in Kapowsin, 9.4 in Graham, 2.5 on South Hill (Puyallup), 5 in Graham, 5 in Eatonville, 1.17 off 128th Street.

It is beyond the scope of this book to go into depth concerning the pros and cons of acquistion, management and sales of realty investments. Let it suffice to say at this point that Ron was proud of his son, Gary, whose one-upmanship found him bettering Ron's game plan.

Gary DeBock, while still single and in his twenties, sold all except one of six rental houses for cash, investing heavily in mobile home lots. Due to such factors as extremely low expenses (about nil) and ease of management, he became increasingly pleased with the investment.

If you know what you are doing, buying and holding houses or lands are better than selling for a commission. In a sense, to sell a rental house is like killing the goose that lays the golden egg.

Admittedly, the data in this chapter hardly merits its

ambitious title. Just chalk it up to an old man dreaming dreams.[170]

Remember this, selling your income properties may give you cash, but holding them might even make you wealthy!

Of course, if that much money pricks your conscience, you might consider your grandchildren or your church.

Epilogue

Did he practice what he preached? No. No, a thousand times no! Oh, it was not because Ron DeBock didn't try. You see, preaching is a narrow art form that gets both its message and authority from the Holy Bible. And that message is: "Be ye perfect, even as your Heavenly Father is perfect."

Since the Word of God covers all matters of life and death, and everything in between and beyond, it did not take Ron long to discover that he fell short of the glory of God. While it was the preaching of John 3:18 by Roy Mourer that brought him to the foot of Calvary, there was enough grace found in Psalm 103:10 to last his lifetime, ...and beyond.

Among those who have lived on earth, only Jesus was sinless. It's not that godliness and perfection should not be preached. They should be preached! Strange as it seems to the individual who has not been introduced to the wonderful Saviour, good works alone — even near perfection — are no ticket to heaven. Perhaps, the bumper sticker puts it best, "Christians are not perfect, just forgiven." Martin Luther caught the futility of mere human efforts to practice what we preach in his classic old hymn, **A Mighty Fortress is our God,** based on Psalm 46:[171]

> Did we in our own strength confide,
> Our striving would be losing;
> Were not the right man on our side,
> the Man of God's own choosing.
>
> Dost ask who that may be?
> Christ Jesus, it is He;
> Lord Sabaoth His name,
> From age to age the same,
> And He must win the battle.

Let the record show, therefore, that Ron preached the whole truth, but that he failed to practice all that he preached.

181

He tried, but he failed. Such failure has always been the basic human experience. Only a keen understanding of God's plan of redemption viewed in juxtaposition with promised rewards for good works can explain such an admission. All have sinned and come short of the glory of God. The striving to be all that the Creator had in mind is honorable motivation, but the bottom line is "...Christ in you, the hope of glory."[172] To deny the "feet of clay" common to the human race is to negate the need for a Savior.[173]

An autobiography forces one to look back. It can be a sobering undertaking. For that matter, **undertaking** is not a bad word to describe the study, since the end result will be rather like an expanded obituary.

One of the most beautiful, fascinating and intriguing aspects of a life led by divine guidance is the way that faith in the unknown pays off in the end. There is no reason we should be surprised at this. In the Old Testament, our example is Abram, who believed implicitly in the Abrahamic Covenant. At age 75, he was instructed by God to leave his country and journey "to a land that I will show you."[174] Abraham's obedient faith led to his walking an uncertain path, with fine-tunings along the way that brought great adventure and abundance to this great patriarch. "And he went out, not knowing where he was going," speaks more of a man who marched to a different drumbeat than of one who plans his life from A to Z.[175]

The New Testament example is St. Paul, who related his conversion experience before Herod Agrippa. Much the same as God had promised to Abram divine guidance for the remaining years of his life, Jesus speaks to Paul in that heavenly vision of a fuller revelation in further appearances as needed.[176]

The significance of the foregoing observations is that any person who accepts Jesus Christ as personal Saviour...
who trusts in the Lord with all his heart,
who will accept the fact that he does not know it all,
who will acknowledge God in all his ways,
...should expect God to direct his paths through life.[177]

On looking back, Ron could not come to any other con-

182

clusion than that the Lord had indeed kept His promises revealed to the teenager at the altar of prayer, seeking direction for life. It all came together. In less than 50 years!

If he had it all to do over again, what would he do differently? Nothing. Being thankful in everything must include all things! But Ron hopes to spend much of his remaining time and energy in helping young people prepare themselves for a life of service. Serving humanity in some way. Preferably in serving the Lord God Almighty.

As a minister in his twenties, Ron often wondered how Christian believers could be satisfied with any vocation other than some phase of ministry. This idea probably grew out of a vision of a Christ who made Himself poor, so that we might become rich.[179] Ron no longer feels quite the same about the matter. However, he still looks for a plausible excuse when encountering a born-again Christian whose highest ambition is merely to make a living. Of course, he gained understanding and tolerance for vocational preferences when it became necessary to change his own course in life from preaching (1950-71) to practicing (1971-present).

Consider the many vocational guidance counselors who stop short of including some form of ministry in the list of possible life endeavors. They will point to the importance of a good education, careful planning, and even willingness to sacrifice. They do not hesitate to advise against low-paying service jobs. They will wear out the line, "Plan your work, then work your plan." But the high calling of pastoral ministry seldom gets honorable mention.

Perhaps it's just as well. Only God calls. And we might add, when God does call, He always equips.

For that matter, God takes delight in anointing some servants whom the world with its lofty wisdom would consider unfit. The humble minister does well to give all the glory to Jesus anyway.

The varied ministries in which Ron was involved proved to be most satisfying personally. Small parishes in the hills, in the country, by the water. He preached to the deaf, to sailors at sea and to fighting U.S. Marines in Vietnam.

Remuneration was never the key issue. A country church provided a parsonage and $60 a week, a welcome improvement upscale from the $10 a week guarantee in the previous place of ministry. Offerings from the deaf churches ranged from about $3 to $25 a Sunday. The reason it was so **large** a sum was because there were two congregations, not one! But God always provided! Donna and Ron never thought of their lack of the finer things in life as a sacrifice. They were serving Almighty God! Take fulness of joy, peace in their hearts and a sense of divine mission: their chosen path of service poured forth many benefits uncommon to most pursuits.

The later years of so-called **practicing** turned out to be a new and different kind of venture. Suppose a layman in a church determines to run his business based upon the Golden Rule and the other Christian principles which he has heard preached in the local church. One may rightly assume that here is a businessman who has an advantage over his unchurched counterpart selling the same product or service. Ron knew well that he had a distinct advantage. Once the decision to launch out into new waters was made, the anticipation became one of sheer excitement. He prepared himself to adhere to a standard of excellence in keeping with the very best. This new venture deserved no less.

Real miracles followed. What encouragement a little miracle now and then can bring into your life! Imagine, for example, finding a furnished house for sale for a full price of $2700 within three miles from where you live, offered to you by a call from a broker, and you discover the lone pair of shoes in the home fit you to a tee! Even more exciting if you just happen to be in the rental house management business. Or imagine that your wife tracks you down to break the news that **a check for you in six figures** has arrived — when you weren't expecting anything from the person who signed it. Or imagine that you finally climb to the top of Mt. Sinai, a lifetime ambition, then only to find that the climb was on the fortieth anniversary of your baptism with the Holy Ghost. What encouragement a little miracle now and then can bring into your life!

Beautiful Puyallup Valley may not be heaven, but it's as close to it Ron will ever get until the real thing comes along. He figures that he was fortunate to have been born and raised in what he considers **God's Country.** Luckier still to return to such a neat place to keep active in later years.

Looking to the future, Ron contemplates a continuation of working with his son, Gary, in property management, of staying active in a local church, and engaging in a ministry...wherever God leads. Keenly aware that there is "only one life, 'twill soon be past, and only what's done for Christ will last," Ron yearns to ride off into the future with the testimony of St. Paul:[180]

"For to me to live is Christ, and to die is gain."

185

Endnotes

1 See 2 Corinthians 5:11.

2 Romans 5:3

3 James 1:5

4 1 Corinthians 15:40, KJV

5 See 2 Timothy 2:15.

6 See John 10:10.

7 Commanding Officer of a ship

8 Destroyer Division 232 was composed of four destroyers.

9 an aircraft carrier

10 time to eat together

11 the room reserved for the officers' mess

12 Executive Officer, the next in command after the Commanding Officer

13 *Encyclopedia Britannica*, 15th ed.

14 demilitarized zone

15 reconnaissance, an exploratory survey to enemy territory to gather information

16 Letter sent from Vietnam, 25 September 1969

17 Viet Cong

18 Matthew 28:18-20, KJV

19 U.S. Navy Commission, 7 June 1971

20 killed in action

21 In Vietnam

22 Reverend Jim Bakker was defrocked on
    6 May 1987. *FORGIVEN* , New York : Atlantic
    Monthly Press, 1989, Charles E . Shepard, 564 .

23 Reverend Richard Dortch was defrocked, but was
    reinstated as a minister of the Assemblies of God on
    20 November 1991. Richard Dortch, *INTEGRITY*,
    1991, New Leaf Press, Inc.

24 Bureau of Naval Personnel Manual

25 Bureau of Naval Personnel

26 See Romans 8:28.

27 See Romans 12:19.

28 T. E. Gannon's letter, 20 November 1970

29 V. J. Lonergan's letter, 7 December 1970

30 See Psalm 23:2.

31 Psalm 91:7, KJV

32 Philippians 1:6b, KJV

33 *Bureau of Naval Personnel Manual*, Article 3830100, paragraph 4.a

34 DeBock's letter to Chairman Gannon, AG Commission on Chaplains, 2 December 1970

35 T. E. Gannon's letter, 9 December 1970

36 Excerpts from column written by Fred Grimm, *Morning News Tribune*, 24 September 1992

37 *Funk and Wagnalls New Standard Bible Dictionary*, Philadelphia: The Blakiston Company

38 Genesis 28:20, 21

39 Harold Street, *The Believer Priest in the Tabernacle Furniture*, 103.

40 James Orr, *The International Standard Bible Encyclopedia*, "Praise" and "to do good and communicate" are called **sacrifices** by the writer of the Epistle to the Hebrews (13:15, 16) . The phrase "believer-priest" is an idea that holds that all believers have a direct approach to God by virtue of their relation to Christ.

41 Lars P. Qualben, *A History of the Christian Church*, 109.

42 *Ibid.*, 109

43 2 Corinthians 5:19

44 John 3:16

45 John 14:13, 14; Acts 3:16; Ephesians 5:20

46 John 3:19-21

47 Romans 10:14

48 Stuart Chase, *The Tyranny of Words*, New York: Harcourt, Brace and Company, 1938, 19.

49 H. G. G. Herklots, *How Our Bible Came to Us,* 12.

50 Philip Schaff, *The Creeds of Christendom*, New York: Harper and Brothers, III, Evangelical Creeds, 4th ed.

51 See the constitutions of states admitted since 1876.

52 John 4:24

53 Oscar Cullman, *Early Christian Worship*, Chicago: Henry Regnery Company, 1953, 12.

54 Arthur S. Hoyt, *Public Worship For Non-Liturgical Churches*, New York: The George H. Doran Company, 1911, 26.

55 Oscar Cullman, *op.cit.*, 20.

56 1 Corinthians 14:26

57 D. Eberhard Nestle, *Novum Testamentum Graece*, New York: American Bible Society, 1950, 304.

58 James Strong, *Dictionary of the Greek New Testament*, New York: Abingdon-Cokesbury Press, 1890, 30.

59 Acts 3:8, 9

60 Luke 19:38

61 Luke 19:40

62 *WEBSTER'S Ninth New Collegiate Dictionary,*
Springfield, Mass.: MERRIAM-WEBSTER INC.

63 *The New International Standard Bible Encyclopedia,*
Chicago: The Howard-Severance Company.

64 C. S. Lewis, *Reflections on the Psalms,* New York:
Harcourt, Brace and Company, 1958, 94.

65 G. S. Bowes as quoted in C. H. Spurgeon, *Treasury of
David,* Grand Rapids, Mich.: Zondervan Publishing
House, ed. by David Otis Fuller, two vols., 1940,
I, 147.

66 H. Orton Wiley, *Christian Theology,* Kansas City,
Missouri: Beacon Hill Press, III, 39.

67 C. H. Spurgeon, *op. cit.,* I, 161.

68 *Ibid.,* I, 173

69 *Ibid.,* II, 100

70 Mark 1:11

71 Luke 21:3

72 Luke 7:9

73 Luke 7:28

74 Alfred B. Smith, *Favorites Number Three,* 13.

75 Luke 19:17

76 Proverbs 12:3; 20:19; 24:24; 29:5

77 Psalm 150:6

78 2 Samuel 22:4

79 Revelation 5:12

80 Psalm 107:8, 15, 21, 31

81 Psalm 103:1

82 Psalm 103:20a

83 Psalm 148:2a

84 Psalm 30:4

85 C. H. Spurgeon, *Treasury of David*, Grand Rapids, Mich.: Zondervan Publishing House, ed. by David O. Fuller, two volumes, 1940, II, 325.

86 Romans 15:11b

87 Psalm 148:12, 13a

88 Psalm 148:11

89 Revelation 19:5

90 Psalm 145:21

91 Psalm 148:3, 7-10

92 Psalm 98:4, 7, 8

93 C. H. Spurgeon, *op. cit.*, I, 226.

94 Isaiah 55:12b

95 Joshua 21:45

96   Compare Hebrews 13:8.

97   1 Chronicles 15:1-29

98   Exodus 15:1-21

99   2 Chronicles 6:1-21

100   Acts 16:25

101   C. H. Spurgeon, *Treasury of David*, Grand Rapids, Mich.: Zondervan Publishing House, ed. by David O. Fuller, two volumes, 1940, II, 53.

102   *Ibid.*, II, 151

103   Psalm 33:1b

104   Matthew 15:8, 9

105   See Ephesians 6:5.

106   1 Chronicles 16:35

107   Psalm 106:47

108   John 10:10

109   1 Peter 1:8

110   Proverbs 23:7

111   Colossians 3:16

112   Psalm 37:4

113   Acts 13:52

114 Psalm 106:2

115 2 Corinthians 9:15

116 Psalm 63:3; 119:171

117 Psalm 51:15; 63:5

118 Ephesians 5:18b-20

119 Psalm 149:1

120 Isaiah 26:19

121 Isaiah 65:14

122 John Wells, *The Morning Exercises*, quoted in C. H. Spurgeon, *Treasury of David*, Grand Rapids, Mich.: Zondervan Publishing House, ed. by David O. Fuller, two volumes, 1940, II, 37.

123 C. H. Spurgeon, *op. cit.*, I, 197.

124 *Ibid.*, II, 64

125 *Ibid.*, II, 100

126 *Ibid.*, I, 144

127 *Ibid.*, I, 161

128 Psalm 95:1

129 C. H. Spurgeon, *op. cit.*, I, 350.

130 *Ibid.*, II, 87

131 2 Chronicles 29:30

132 2 Chronicles 30:21

133 Henry H. Halley, *Best Bible Verses*, Box 774,
     Chicago 90, Illinois: n. d., 601.

134 *Ibid.*, 643

135 2 Chronicles 20:6, 7

136 Acts 16:25

137 1Thessalonians 5:17

138 Romans 12:15

139 See Paul's personal testimony before Agrippa in
     Acts 26.

140 Psalm 47:1

141 C. H. Spurgeon, *Treasury of David*, Grand Rapids,
     Mich.: Zondervan Publishing House, ed. by
     David O. Fuller, two volumes, 1940, I, 162.

142 C. H. Spurgeon, *op. cit.*, II, 335.

143 *Ibid.*,

144 Psalm 40:3

145 James Orr, *The International Standard Bible
     Encyclopaedia*, Chicago: The Howard-Severance
     Company. See also Exodus 15:20ff and
     2 Samuel 6:5-14.

146 Luke 2:14; Ephesians 5:19; Colossians 3:16;
     Revelation 5:9

147 Psalm 51:17

148 Job 51:17

149 Helen P. Strong, *The Garment of Praise*, copyrighted 1888 by The American Tract Society, pamphlet, 27.

150 See page 65 of this book.

151 C. S. Lewis, *Reflections on the Psalms*, New York: Harcourt, Brace and Company, 1958, 94.

152 Hebrews 12:14; 1 Peter 1:16

153 Colossians 3:22-24

154 James 4:7, 8, KJV

155 Reverend Sam Benson, quoted from his sermon at Puyallup First Assembly, 6 December 1992

156 John 2:1-11

157 Acts 20:35

158 Mark 8:35

159 Matthew 23:11

160 See John 5:39 and 2 Timothy 2:15.

161 Mark 8:35-37, TLB

162 Matthew 4:4, KJV

163 Ward M. Tanneberg, *Let Light Shine Out*, 1977, 77.

164 John 3:16, KJV

165 *The Pierce County Herald*, 16 October 1992

166 *The Pierce County Herald*, 8 February 1992

167 This list of words appeared in *The Wheel*, weekly bulletin of The Rotary Club of Puyallup, 7 October 1992.

168 Proverbs 30:8b-9a, KJV

169 See page 121 for additional information on realty investments.

170 See Joel 2:28.

171 Gospel Publishing House, Springfield, MO, 1969, *Hymns of Glorious Praise.*

172 Colossians 1:27

173 Daniel 2:33

174 Genesis 12:1, NKJV

175 Hebrews 11:8, NKJV

176 See Acts 26:16.

177 See Proverbs 3:5-6.

178 See 1 Thessalonians 5:18.

179 See 2 Corinthians 8:9.

180 Philippians 1:21, KJV

Appendix

A. Letters to Ron

B. Poetry by Ron

C. Adult Class Notes

D. Ron's Revised Resumé

WASHINGTON

NORTHERN IDAHO

Northwest District Council
OF THE
Assemblies of God
Incorporated

DWIGHT H. McLAUGHLIN, Superintendent

RALPH M. PHILLIPS, Secretary-Treasurer

| 230 CHURCHES | 540 MINISTERS | 92 FOREIGN MISSIONARIES |

DISTRICT PRESBYTERS

W. H. BOYLES
Spokane, Wash.

HUGH D. CANTELON
Port Angeles, Wash.

MERLE A. GLEW
Seattle, Wash.

KENNETH GREGG
Chelan, Wash.

R. E. MADER
Pullman, Wash.

E. M. McLAUGHLIN
Yakima, Wash.

W. F. MORTON
Kelso, Wash.

M. S. OSS
Everett, Wash.

E. R. SCRATCH
Olympia, Wash.

E. H. TIGNER
Tacoma, Wash

•

GENERAL PRESBYTERS

R. J. CARLSON
Spokane, Wash.

W. F. MORTON
Kelso, Wash.

•

MISSIONARY SEC'Y

W. W. FLEMING
Sunnyside, Wash.

•

**CHRIST'S AMBASSADOR
& SUNDAY SCHOOL
DIRECTOR**

VERNON W. SKAGGS
Seattle, Wash.

•

**NORTHWEST BIBLE
COLLEGE**
Seattle, Wash.

C. E. BUTTERFIELD
President

A Training School For
Ministers and
Missionaries

Operated jointly with
the Montana District
Council

•

**NORTHWEST
DISTRICT MESSENGER**

Official Organ of the
Northwest District
Council

Executive Offices
VErmont 3880

435 East 72nd Street
Seattle 5, Washington

April 16, 1953.

Ronald G. DeBock,
13742 30th N.E.,
Seattle 55, Wash.

Dear Brother DeBock:

    Choice greetings in the Name of our Lord!

    It is with pleasure that I inform you that the Credentials Committee of the Northwest District Council has approved you for full ordination with the General Council of the Assemblies of God.

    Therefore it will be necessary for you to be present at the Ordination service to be held at Bethany Temple, Everett, Washington on April 24, 1953 at 7:30 p.m.

    There will be forms for you to fill out immediately after the Ordination service, so please do not leave the service until you have contacted me. It is necessary for you to be present to be ordained and if you cannot be present, you will have to wait until the next Council meeting.

    The sincerest prayers of the entire District Presbytery are with you and they will welcome your inquiries and be most happy to counsel with you in any of your problems and rejoice with you in your victories. Feel free to call on them at any time.

    We shall expect you in Everett on April 24th at 7:30 p.m.

Sincerely yours in the Lord,

Ralph M. Phillips,
Secretary

200

Illinois District Council, Assemblies of God

P. O. BOX 323 • CARLINVILLE, ILLINOIS 62626 • (217) 854-3261

RICHARD W. DORTCH
SUPERINTENDENT

April 14, 1971

Ronald Gene DeBock, Lietenant Commander
Chaplain Corps, U.S.N.R.
2539 North Meridian Dr.F V
Naval Training Center
Great Lakes, Illinois   60088

Dear Brother DeBock:

Choice Christian greetings!

Thank you for your letter. We certainly do want you to come to our District Council and to bring us about 10 or 15 minutes of what God is doing for you in your work. As I mentioned to you, we need exposure in this area of ministry.

We would like for you to be ready Wednesday morning at about 9:30, May 5th.

Anything we can do to help you, let us know. Most of us will be staying at the Lewis and Clark Motel in East Alton, Illinois.

Looking forward to seeing you.

In Christ,
Your brother,

Richard W. Dortch
District Superintendent

GENERAL COUNCIL OF THE ASSEMBLIES OF GOD
1445 BOONVILLE AVENUE
SPRINGFIELD, MISSOURI 65802

THOS. F. ZIMMERMAN
GENERAL SUPERINTENDENT

April 15, 1971

Chaplain, LCDR Ronald Gene DeBock
2539 No. Meridian Dr., FV
Naval Training Center
Great Lakes, Illinois 60088

Dear Ron:

Warmest Greetings!

Please accept our very best wishes on your having been given an honorable discharge from the United States Navy, as well as the disability severance which is proper in recognition of the injuries incurred in Vietnam. We know this has been a matter of grave concern to you. We are thankful to the Lord that He has resolved this in a way that will give full recognition for the years of faithful service which you have rendered and will put you in a position to look to the future with a sense of assurance and security.

I just wanted you to know of my pleasure in the way this matter has been resolved.

We wish you well and assure you of our earnest prayers that God may guide you in all of your way.

Sincerely yours,

Thos. F. Zimmerman
General Superintendent

TFZ:vl
cc: T. E. Gannon

11-21-87

The Vikings Won Their Game Last Night

The Vikings won their game last night
(They clobbered ol' Kelso!)
I shouted till my throat was sore
Like forty years ago!

But I ask, "Isn't life like that a lot
When you take on a 'ten and oh'"(10-0)
If you believe in yourself and what you've got
You can conquer any foe!

I jumped and I raved…(You knew I would!)
…As our score began to grow.
To get on top makes us feel so good!
(Who yearns for the "status quo?")

Yes, life's like that: you're up; you're down.
Will your project really go?
When you get the ball, will you give it your all
And hit your man with your throw?

Work at it with sweat, and what'll you get
As the years may come and go?
Hard to say, but this I'll bet:
You'll reap just what you sow!

If you're determined to heighten the joys of life
This one thing I know:
You'll reckon the struggle, the knocks and the strife
Were eclipsed by the love you could show.

by Ron DeBock

"VIKINGS, FIRST IN THE STATE"
by Ron DeBock, class of '46

First in the state; Our team was great!
The trophy's in our lap.
OK, you fans, let's celebrate,
P U Y A L L U P's on the map!

They had but one aim: To win the game
As the Vikings went out on the grid.
And Puyallup will never be the same,
'Cause they woke up the town when they did!

Now, P U Y A L L U P's a name that's hard to pronounce
And tougher, yet, to rhyme,
But follow the ball and watch it bounce
And you'll get it right every time.

Oh, the top is so sweet, As Gonzaga you beat
Now, enjoy the fame and the fun!
'Cause when the Bullpups barked and went down in defeat
You Vikings emerged No. ONE!

Most fans are too frail, too old or too weak
To line up with the team on the field.
Thank God, they didn't need a great physique
When they cheered, when they yelled, when they squealed!

"It's only a game? There is no real fame?
You question the pain and the cost?
I remind you that life as a whole is the same
If you can't reach your goal, you have lost.

So if you should meet an alum on the street
And notice the smile on his face,
He feels so neat, so good and upbeat
'Cause the Vikings have captured first place!

First in the state; Our team was great!
PUYALLUP's on the go;
OK, you fans, let's celebrate,
Toss the ball to Mayor Crowe.

204

LISTEN TO HIM!

Lonely here, but feeling gr...8,

I'm eating salami on a paper pl...8.

Sorry I'm not with my m...8;

That seldom happens; she's never l...8!

Excited, though, I must rel...8

Numbers copied by those who sk...8

Thrice appear this very d...8:

One dash 8 dash 8 and 8.

Hearken to your God. Don't hesit...8.

If you Listen to Him, I don't exagger...8,

My salami will be tasty like the famed blue pl...8!

(Because I love you, I encourage you to medit...8)

by Ron DeBock
written 1-8-88

My Inspiration . . . Donna

Days go by...and months and years
These eyes of mine fill now with tears
Neglected thanks and contemplation
Have left untold appreciation.

My Dear, I was the richest groom
Across the threshold to one room.
You ne'er complained the real privation
While hubby got his education.

Reflecting on those schoolhood days
'Twas you, Dear, who deserved the praise!
You went without the whole duration
So I might get a good foundation.

Little Bev made her debut
Blessed companionship for you.
She came to cheer our humble station
And brought her daddy much elation.

Gary next - at last a son!
The doctor said to me, "Well done!"
Hand shakes and "Congratulations!"
The girl and boy were His creation.

Little Janny with her eyes
Blue, of course, but bigger size.
This completes the delegation
To our family relation.

Looking back I see the price:
Your patience, love and sacrifice.
And, if my gratitude I ration
It's been neglect and not negation!

by Ron DeBock
- approx 1960

A Son Who Makes Me Proud

I arose quite early this morning
To scratch out some lines on my pad
Because on my mind has been "dawning"
That my boy has been making me glad.

"Like father, like son," I've heard them remark
When comparing a boy with his dad;
But since the son has shown more spark:
I wish it were true, I might add!

It's great to know the Lord and be free
In a land where God meets every need;
With a son like mine in the family tree,
The gladness is treasured indeed.

Far better than money in the bank
As I'm gradually growing old,
Is this treasured son for whom God I do thank
More cherished than silver or gold.

Now don't think I get all the credit
For raising this marvelous lad!
But it's just as Solomon said it,
"A wise son makes a father so glad." (Prov. 10:1)

This son whose studies have been so intense
And whose lifestyle of uncommon thrift,
Has, by refusing even normal expense,
Become to his dad a great gift.

For example, the Navy was home to them both,
And studies for status and gain;
While dad got the stripes and degrees for his work,
His son clearly excelled in the brain.

And now that son will take on a wife:
(He announced that he plans to marry).
I'm convinced that great blessing will come to his life
When Ruth joins in wedlock with Gary.

No matter what happens to me as I roam
I'll thank my dear God up above
For a son who has turned my mere house into "home,"
And filled this heart with unmerited love.

by Ron DeBock in 1989

Clean Inside Again*
Lyrics by Ron DeBock

Here at the altar now
Humbly again I bow
And feel so clean inside again.

I have been here before
And I'll be back some more
To feel I'm clean inside again!

His arms are open wide,
In comes the cleansing tide.
I feel so clean inside again!

Through tears I sought His grace:
Would He my sins erase
And make me clean inside again?

His arms are open wide,
In comes the cleansing tide.
I feel so clean inside again!

Through tears I found His grace:
Jesus, Who took my place
And made me clean inside again.

* These words were written to be sung to the melody of a popular love song. Can you guess which one?

208

*Touch of Calvary**
Lyrics by Ron DeBock

In the past Thou hast dealt with me
Till at last I touched Calvary.
Oh, my God, my soul doth long to be
Aware again of all that touch
Once did for me!

It's not much to ask that men seek Thee.
Just one touch and they, too, will be free.
Oh, my God, my soul doth long to be
Aware again of all that touch
Once did for me!

Some I've met have called my faith in vain
But how can I forget the day you called my name?
Oh, my God, my soul doth long to be
Aware again of all that touch
Once did for me!

On the cross was nailed all my care.
Yet where's the loss? I'm called a millionaire.
Oh, my God, my soul doth long to be
Aware again of all that touch
Once did for me!

Now my years are almost at an end.
And through the tears I see my truest Friend!
Oh, my God, my soul doth long to be
Aware again of all that touch
Once did for me!

* These words were written to be sung to a melody which was allegedly the Number One tune in Vietnam in 1965, a haunting melody still remembered.

FAMILY LIFE EDUCATION
Adult Class, Chapel
Creating Your World With Words
Ron DeBock, Teacher

THE WORD OF GOD...

...in the heart

...on the tongue

Where have we gone astray?

The world has its own language. The big problem is that the believers hear the world and speak as the world speaks. We know that there is true authority of the Word, but the body of Christ has failed to live in that available authority!

To be effective, men must hide the Word of God away in the heart. All else will follow...but not without practice. And it will not happen just because we memorize Scripture. Meditation upon the Word of God cannot be overemphasized as an important point of beginning. It is a matter of substituting God's Word(s) for those of the enemy of our soul!

The Word(s) of Jesus found in our Bible, are not merely **written Words,** they are **alive evermore!**

Live in the authority of the Word!

Christians should be different from the world...and their language will be noticeably different, too. For example, the believer ought to be using uplifting, up-beat, positive words. He should never be a complainer! Why not? Simply because we are enjoined to "Always be joyful. No matter what happens, **always be thankful,** for this is God's will for you who belong to Christ Jesus." – I Thess. 5:16, 18, The Living Bible

God's Word is **creative power.** That creative power is produced by the heart, formed by the tongue, and released out of the mouth in word form.

We need to learn to confess **victory** in the face of apparent defeat. We need to confess **abundance** in the face of apparent lack.

Will you look with me again at a verse of Scripture which you have read a hundred or more times before? It is from Mark 11:23...

"...whosoever shall SAY TO THIS

MOUNTAIN , 'Be thou removed,' ..."

What do you see now as you read the promise which Jesus made? See that Jesus is not asking for prayer here. A prayer is to God. This is not one of those! Not at all. Instead, this is the way/procedure which our Lord Jesus advises when a real obstacle confronts us...when a real **mountain-of-a- problem** stands in our path! Are we to be whipped? Is there no way out? Must we admit defeat? Absolutely not! **Speak to the problem itself!!!**

FAMILY LIFE EDUCATION
Adult Class, Chapel
Creating Your World With Words
Ron DeBock, Teacher

FAITH WITH WORKS IS PERFECTED

But when it is without works, it is dead--that is, **rejected!**
- James 2:22, 26

OK, then, if the works are not forthcoming, what's the problem?

Why not approach this nagging question by asking another? "When my prayers **were answered** what were the circumstances?"

More importantly, **what is the missing ingredient** which must be present in faith for the works, signs and wonders to follow?

Fortunately for believers, there is no scarcity of biblical instruction on faith and no scarcity of biblical examples of faith rewarded! Nevertheless, there seems to be a lack of the **works of faith** among Christians today. What we need is both a review of the broad principles of faith, and some **fine-tuning of faith** and how it works to produce works!

8 8 8 8 8 8 8 8 8 8 8 8 8 8 8 8 8 8 8 8 8 8 8 8 8 8 8 8 8 8 8

SPEAK FAITH WORDS TO YOUR NEED

Creativity is your privilege as a child of the Creator! Incidentally, if you don't believe this...it would not be difficult for you to convince me that (for you) the statement is indeed without significance.

"...What things soever ye desire when ye pray, believe that ye receive them, and ye shall have them."   Mark 11:24

"...(faith) is the evidence of things not seen."   Hebrews 11:1b

"For let not that man (that wavereth) think that he shall receive anything of the Lord. "...ye have not, because ye ask not. Ye ask, and re-receive not, because ye ask amiss..."   James 1:7; 4:2-3

"If ye abide in me, and my words abide in you, ye shall ask what ye will, and it shall be done unto you."   John 15:7

"Ask and it shall be given you; seek, and ye shall find; knock, and it shall be opened unto you..."   Matthew 7:7

** **

THE ANSWER YOU DESIRE IS WAITING FOR YOU!   YES..

Yes, this the plain and simple truth found in the Word! But, guess what. Something was still missing! Let's make a check-off list like they do down at Jiffy Lube:

This thing/answer I need...Do I really want it? Is it my earnest desire? Am I fervent in my prayer?

Do I really believe that God will reward me? Am I ready to zero in? Am I white hot? Do I really intend to "go for it?"

Am I intense? Is it the "one thing I desire & will seek after?" Does it fit into God's perfect will for my life? Is there nothing wavering?

Is there agreement in the Word, truly unselfish? Am I convinced I will hear the divine "YES?"
Have I lost sleep? shed tears? worked hard? sweat? invested time? money? intensity?
Or...have a succumbed to the devil's lie: mediocre is OK, average is normal, not worth the pain.

Practice What You Preached

FAMILY LIFE EDUCATION
Adult Class, Chapel
Creating Your World With Words
Ron DeBock, Teacher

THE TRIUNE TREASURE TROVE

Now hear this...and listen well! If you simply believe as you prayerfully go
for something...**yes, anything**...you will do well to dust off the shelf where
that thing will go...because (despite all the doubters out there who are only
too happy to discourage you) you will very soon see the thing you prayed for!

> **"Listen to me! You can pray for anything, and if you can believe, you have it;
> I T ' S   Y O U R S ! "**
> - Mark 11:24 The Living Bible

Suppose, for example, you've decided you have waited long enough. You want to
be baptized with the Holy Ghost and fire. Then search the Scriptures, study
the whole matter, go to God in prayer, believe...and simply **RECEIVE!!**

Or suppose you would like to serve as an usher in the church, sing in the choir, teach a
Sunday School class or volunteer for bagging groceries in the Benevolence department. Simply let
your **desire be made known (with words)** to the pastor once you are convinced God is leading you in
such endeavor.

But you say, Ron, suppose I want something like a new job or travel or suppose I really
dream about getting a college degree. Does the promise in Mark 11:24 extend to such things? All
I hear you saying is serving the Lord or the church. I have some aspirations of my own!

LIKE ANY OF THESE?

a brand new car   a fine home of my own so I won't have to pay rent   so much
cash in my savings that I will tell the bank manager that I like this bank, but regret that since
only $100,000 of my deposit is insured by FDIC, I must transfer some of my savings to other banks

**a trip to the Holy Land   travel to some islands in the Pacific (for sunshine & recreation)
a trip to visit the largest church in the world where Paul Cho is the pastor in Seoul, Korea, and
get a picture of me at his desk   a trip to Cairo to see the pyramids and ride a camel!**

I want a business of my own, but not one that will tie me down too much. It must provide
a rather substantial income (so that my tithe can average above $25,000 annually). I also desire
steady income from such sources as writings, commissions, real estate contracts & Social Security.

**I would like to be recognized in the academic field...get a masters degree and a doctor's degree,
teach in a university, publish a book.   I'd like to be cited by my alma mater.   I would like
my picture to appear on the front page of The Pentecostal Evangel!**

OR SOME OF THESE?

My personal physician will inform me that my health is excellent and I should continue to watch
my diet and get plenty of exercise regularly.   I want a grandfather's clock.   I want
a new set of Encyclopedia Britannica!   I would like more free time...say, about a week each
month so I can do what I want, like relax, travel or just read books in the park.

I desire one of those giant screen tv sets, so I can really enjoy sports at home!

What I really would like is some sweet little grandkids to play with, but I don't want them to
live too far away (or we could not visit easily).   I'd also like a beautiful rose garden,
but am too busy to spend time caring for it. (Perhaps my wife would like to keep it up??) I'd
like a maintenance company to do my yard work, too, except I want to do **a little for exercise!**

I would like to become an ordained minister of my denomination. I want a real challenge
such as a ministry in combat situations with some military units, like some had in Vietnam! Oh,
yes, and I'd like to be able to fit into my uniform on Military Recognition Sunday in my church.

**I want to be specific in my prayers and get answers daily! I'd like to experience measurable
blessings in my life such as seeing the hand of God move on a certain day of each week...such as
Tuesday! I would like "surprises" from the hand of God -- that is, unexpected things happening
FOR WHICH I HAVE NOT PRAYED, BUT WHICH MY WONDERFUL LORD SIMPLY GIVES TO ME ANYWAY SINCE HE LOVES
TO SEE ME PROSPER.**

212

FAMILY LIFE EDUCATION
Adult Class, Chapel
Ron DeBock, Instructor

A LABORATORY COMPARISON

F L O W I N G   S T R E A M S   I N   T H E   G O D H E A D
A N D   I N   T H E   C R E A T E D   T I M E - U N I V E R S E

G o d	U n i v e r s e	T i m e

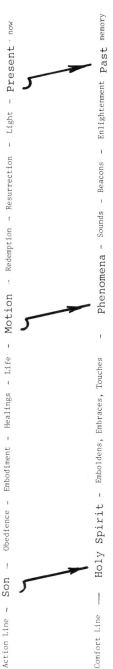

The SOURCE Father — Reservoir — Love — Wisdom · Primal — Energy · Starting Point — Beginning — Future · Genesis

Action Line – Son :: Obedience – Embodiment – Healings – Life – Motion · Redemption – Resurrection – Light – Present · now

Comfort Line — Holy Spirit – Emboldens, Embraces, Touches — Phenomena – Sounds – Beacons – Enlightenment Past memory

The BENEFICIARY

Believers/The Church   All Mankind
"whoever believes in Him..."   "whoever desires..."
John 3:16 (NKJV)   Rev. 22:17 (NKJV)

213

PREPARATION

Education:

A. Academic Degrees: B.A. A.A. M.Div. Ph.D.

Bachelor of Arts, Northwest College, Kirkland, WA 1953
Master of Divinity, Western Evangelical Seminary, 1960
    Portland, OR
Associate in Arts, Tacoma Community College, 1979
    Tacoma, WA
Doctor of Philosophy, California Graduate School 1979
    of Theology, Glendale, CA

B. Other Education:

Puyallup High School, graduated   1946
University of Puget Sound, pre-Medicine course   1948-49
Christian Writer's Institute, correspondence course 1952
University of Washington   1952, 66-67
Long Beach City College   1962-63
Army Education Center, Okinawa   1964
University of Maryland, Tokyo, Japanese language 1968

C. Elementary and Secondary:

Garfield Elementary, Olympia, WA   1934-35
Washington Grade School, Olympia, WA   1935-38
Lincoln Elementary, Olympia, WA   1938-39
Orting Grade School, Orting, WA   1939-40
Puyallup Junior High, Puyallup, WA   1940-41
South Bay Elementary, Olympia, WA   1941-42
Queen Anne High School, Seattle, WA   1942-43
Puyallup High School, Puyallup, WA   1943-44
Olympia High School, Olympia, WA   1944-45
Puyallup High School, Puyallup, WA   1945-46

PREACHING

Ministerial Experience

A. Military Chaplaincy (U. S. Navy)
Naval Training Center, Great Lakes, Illinois	1970-71
Third Marine Division, Okinawa, R. I., Japan	1970
Third Marine Division, Vietnam	1969-70
Marine Corps Air Station, Iwakuni, Japan	1967-69
Naval Supply Depot, Seattle, Washington	1965-67
Third Marine Division, Da Nang, Vietnam	1965
Third Marine Division, Okinawa, R. I., Japan	1964-65
Naval Air Station, Memphis, Tennessee	1963-64
Destroyer Division 232, Long Beach, California	1960-61
Chaplains School, Newport, Rhode Island	1959
USN & USMC Recruit Training Center, Portland, Oregon	1958
Bremerton Naval Shipyard, Bremerton, Washington	1958

B. Churches (Northwest District, Assemblies of God)
Lakebay Community Church, Lakebay, Washington	1954-57
Longbranch Community Church, Longbranch, Washington	1954-57
Assembly of God, Montesano, Washington	1953
Assembly of God, Mineral, Washington	1953
Seattle Deaf Assembly, Seattle, Washington	1950-53
Tacoma Deaf Assembly, Tacoma, Washington	1951-53

PRACTICING

A. Awards:
from Northwest College, Kirkland, Washington:

"Delta Epsilon Chi Honor Society"	1992
"President's Award" (see page 217)	1988
"Alumnus of the Year"	1966-67

from military service (Navy and Marine Corps):
Presidential Unit Citation
World War II Victory Medal
National Defense Service Medal
Armed Forces Reserve Medal
Vietnam Service Medal with 3 Stars and
      Combat Operations Insignia
Vietnam Campaign Medal with Device
Vietnam Cross of Gallantry with Palm

B. Business:
Rainier Rentals, founder/owner, residential management firm
    located in Puyallup, WA since 1975. Gary DeBock, Ron's
    son, became General Manager in 1990.

C. Certificates and Memberships:

Rotary International, Puyallup Club	since	1990
Real Property Assessment Certificate, WA state		1978
Washington Association of REALTORS, Inc.		1952&76
Kiwanis, Puyallup Club		1975
Puyallup Chamber of Commerce		1975
Lieutenant Commander, US Naval Reserve		1971
Military Chaplains Association of the USA	since	1958
Veterans of Foreign Wars	life member	
Disabled American Veterans	life member	
Puyallup First Assembly	since	1946
General Council of the Assemblies of God		
	ordained minister since	1953
Northwest District Council of the Assemblies of God		
	licensed to preach	1950

PRESIDENT'S AWARD

Citation

Dr. Ronald G. DeBock

Dr. Ron DeBock graduated from Northwest College with his Bachelor of Arts in 1953. He received his Master of Divinity Degree from Western Evangelical Seminary in 1960 and his PH. D. from California Graduate School in 1979. He also has additional education at Tacoma Community College where he received an A. A. Degree in 1979, the University of Washington in 1952 and 1966, Long Beach City College in 1962, and the University of Maryland in 1964.

Ron has been affiliated with the College in a number of different ways having served as its Public Relations Director, honored as its Alumnus of the Year, and most recently has distinguished himself as member of the Funding and Endowment Board of Northwest College. Dr. DeBock currently is the owner of Rainier Rentals, a real estate management company in Puyallup, Washington, and is active at Puyallup First Assembly of God as well as serving on the Board at Northwest Teen Challenge.

Dr. Ronald G. DeBock is being honored with the President's Award from Northwest College for his service on the Funding and Endowment Board. Through personal contacts of Dr. DeBock's substantial endowment fund gifts have been generated for Northwest College. Not only did Dr. DeBock play an important role in the college receiving large endowment gifts from third parties, he, himself, has led as an example by making a sizeable contribution to the Endowment Fund. Dr. DeBock also served as a Centurion for many years, showing his commitment to the annual giving drive of the College.

In recognition of the significant service and contributions to Northwest College and its Funding and Endowment Board, President D. V. Hurst, upon approval of the Board of Directors honors Dr. Ronald G. DeBock with the President's Award.

217

Index

How To Order Copies of This Book

FIREBALL PUBLICATIONS   (206) 848-5873
422 W. Main
Puyallup, WA 98371

Please send me _____ copies of **Practice What You Preached.** I am ENCLOSING $ _____ (please add 75¢ per copy for handling). Send check or money order — no cash or C.O.D.'s. Please allow 4 weeks for delivery.

Order at your local bookstore, by mail using this form or by FAX (206) 845-7845.

First edition softcover ordered by mail   **$9.95** each
Second edition hardcover ordered by mail   **$19.95** each
Washington residents add sales tax unless exempt.
Prices subject to change without notice.

Prepaid church order discounts:
over 11 copies … 10%
over 22 copies … 20%
over 44 copies … 30%

Prepaid bookstore quantity discounts up to 40%. Please order by FAX.

PLEASE

PRINT

OR

TYPE

| Mr.   Mrs. |
| (circle one) |
| Ms.   Miss |
| Name _____ |
| Address _____ |
| City _____ State _____ Zip _____ |

Notes

Notes

Notes

Notes

Notes

Notes

Notes

Notes

Notes